D0886758

Hudson Area Public Library
DISCARD
Hudson, Illinois 61748

DISCARD

Theodore Roosevelt
26th President of the United States

Rebecca Stefoff

 GARRETT EDUCATIONAL CORPORATION

Hudson Area Public Library
DISCARD
Hudson, Illinois 61748

Cover: *Official presidential portrait of Theodore Roosevelt by John Singer Sargent.* (Copyrighted by the White House Historical Association; photograph by the National Geographic Society.)

Copyright © 1989 by Garrett Educational Corporation

All rights reserved including the right of reproduction in whole or in part in any form without the prior written permission of the publisher. Published by Garrett Educational Corporation, 130 East 13th Street, P.O. Box 1588, Ada, Oklahoma 74820.

Manufactured in the United States of America

Edited and produced by Synthegraphics Corporation

Library of Congress Cataloging in Publication Data
Stefoff, Rebecca, 1951–
  Theodore Roosevelt, 26th president of the United States.

  (Presidents of the United States)
  Bibliography: p.
  Includes index.
  Summary: Describes the childhood, education, employment, and political career of the energetic man who served as the twenty-sixth president of the United States.
  1. Roosevelt, Theodore, 1858–1919 – Juvenile literature. 2. Presidents – United States – Biography – Juvenile literature. [1. Roosevelt, Theodore, 1858–1919. 2. Presidents] I. Title. II. Title: Theodore Roosevelt, twenty-sixth president of the United States. III. Series.
  E757.S86 1988 973.91'1'0924 [B] [92] 87-35953
  ISBN 0-944483-09-7

13293

Contents

Chronology for
Theodore Roosevelt

1858 Born on October 27 in New York City

1880 Graduated from Harvard College; married Alice Hathaway Lee on October 27

1882– 1884 Served as representative in New York state legislature and became leader of a group of reform-minded Republicans

1884 Alice Roosevelt died on February 14 after birth of daughter

1886 Ran for mayor of New York City but was not elected; married Edith Kermit Carow on December 2

1889– 1895 Served as a member of the U.S. Civil Service Commission

1897– 1898 Served as assistant secretary of the U.S. Navy

1898 Colonel of Rough Riders, a volunteer cavalry regiment in the Spanish-American War in Cuba; led action near San Juan Hill

1899– 1900 Served as governor of New York

1900 Elected Vice-President under President William McKinley

1901– 1905 As 26th President of the United States, after McKinley's assassination, made Panama Canal Treaty and started antitrust movement

1905– **1909**	Second term as President; won Nobel Peace Prize; continued antitrust activities
1909– **1910**	African expedition and wildlife safari; trip to Europe
1912	Survived assassination attempt; defeated as presidential candidate of Progressive Party
1913– **1914**	Explored River of Doubt in Brazil
1919	Died on January 15 at Sagamore Hill, New York

Strong-minded, vigorous, and fiercely patriotic, President Theodore Roosevelt guided the United States to a place of leadership among the nations of the world. (Library of Congress.)

Chapter 1

The Charge of the Rough Riders

It was July 1 in the year 1898. Since April, the United States had been at war with Spain. Now, in the Pacific Ocean, the U.S. Navy was fighting to seize the tiny island of Guam and the much larger island chain called the Philippines from Spanish control. The war was also being fought in newspapers and at social affairs in Washington and Madrid, as the two nations issued informal insults and formal declarations.

The Spanish-American War actually started in the Caribbean, on the Spanish-held island of Cuba, where fighting had been going on for several months. There, on that first day of July, an unusual hero entered American history.

The Americans were making an all-out attack on Santiago de Cuba, the biggest city on the island's southeast coast. But the city was protected by a Spanish fortress atop a high ridge called San Juan Hill. From this position, the Spanish troops fired down upon the several U.S. Army regiments that were massing to assault the ridge from below. The regular Army, however, was not the only American force in Cuba that day.

VOLUNTEERS AGAINST SPAIN

At the beginning of the war, President William McKinley had authorized the formation of several groups of volunteer cavalrymen, or horse-mounted soldiers, to assist the regular Army. The First U.S. Volunteer Cavalry Regiment was known as the Rough Riders; the regiment won its nickname because it included many rugged cowboys from the western states, as well as a few adventurous easterners.

The Rough Riders were supposed to have horses, but a shortage of space on the troop transport ship that carried them to Cuba had forced them to leave their mounts behind in Florida. Only the officers of the regiment had horses. Now the Rough Riders were among other U.S. forces encamped at the foot of San Juan Hill on July 1. They were hoping that the coming assault would successfully carry them through the deadly hail of Spanish rifle fire to the top of the hill.

Suddenly, the signal to advance was given. And the colonel who was the second in command of the Rough Riders led his men off with a wild war whoop. Fired with enthusiasm by their leader, the Rough Riders surged in a rapid, unexpected charge up the slopes of Kettle Hill, a large hill that stood to one side of San Juan Hill. The colonel and his valiant volunteers swarmed up Kettle Hill and seized the small Spanish outpost there. Then the colonel looked across the open valley between Kettle Hill and San Juan Hill. Without hesitation, he led a headlong charge across the valley, exposed to enemy fire.

Although only a handful of his men followed at first, the colonel rode back and forth through the rain of bullets, urging on both his own Rough Riders and the regular Army regiments that had joined the attack. And he won the day. The wild rush that had carried him and his followers up Kettle Hill, seemingly oblivious to danger, had shaken the Spanish defenders and weakened their fighting spirit. Before the

Pictures like this one, showing the charge of the Rough Riders up San Juan Hill, made the sword-brandishing Roosevelt a national hero after the Spanish-American War. In reality, most of the Rough Riders ran up the hill; their horses had been left behind in Florida. (Library of Congress.)

day was over, San Juan Hill had fallen to the Americans. The city of Santiago de Cuba followed two weeks later.

THE HERO OF SAN JUAN HILL

Excited war reporters filled American newspapers with accounts of the charge up San Juan Hill. (Kettle Hill was actually overlooked in most popular accounts of the battle, probably because its name seemed much less romantic.) Every report heaped praise on the colonel who had led the charge of the Rough Riders. He had rallied his own and other troops to assault the heavily defended hill; he had killed at least one of the enemy with a swing of his sword; and he had gone on doggedly urging the attack after receiving a wound in one elbow. The commanding officer of the Rough Riders, Major General Leonard Wood, described the colonel's charge as "very desperate and extremely gallant." Who was this hero?

He was a 39-year-old New Yorker who had been an amateur scientist, a gentleman boxer, a law student, a politician, and a cowboy—but who had never had any military training or experience. He was an exceptionally vigorous, robust man. About five feet, eight inches tall, he weighed nearly 200 pounds, mostly muscle. He had a great barrel chest, a thick neck, and broad shoulders. His brown hair was cut short, but his moustache was long and bushy. People who met him remembered the jovial impression formed by his lively blue eyes (he usually wore pince-nez, a type of spectacles that clipped to the nose), his toothy grin, and his booming laugh.

His name was Theodore Roosevelt, Jr. At the outbreak of the Spanish-American War, he was known to only a few Americans as the assistant secretary of the Navy. After the first of July, however, he was known far and wide as the hero of San Juan Hill. And in little more than three years, the impetuous charge that had carried Theodore Roosevelt up the Cuban hillside would also carry him to the White House.

Chapter 2
A Very Respectable Family

This volunteer colonel with the colorful background came from one of America's oldest families. The first of Roosevelt's ancestors to come to America was a farmer and trader named Claes Maertenzen von Rosenvelt, who, in the 17th century, sailed from his native Holland to the Dutch colony of New Netherlands in the New World. In 1644, he arrived in the small town of New Amsterdam. After the long, uncomfortable sea voyage from Europe, it is easy to imagine von Rosenvelt leaning across the rail of the tall sailing ship as it glided into the harbor, drinking in the moist breezes from the surrounding forests and gazing eagerly at the wooden houses and patchwork fields of his new homeland.

New Amsterdam, a settlement of several hundred people on Manhattan Island, was the heart of Dutch activity in the New World. In 1609, the Englishman Henry Hudson, working for the Dutch East India Company, had explored the region and opened it for trade. Now New Amsterdam was the commercial center of a wide area, reaching far up the Hudson River into what would later become New York State. The American colonies were growing, as first exploration and then settlement pushed ever farther into new territory. A hard-working and shrewd person could prosper in this New World, and von Rosenvelt was both.

Before long, the von Rosenvelt family had achieved some importance in the community. The family name was changed to Roosevelt, perhaps simply by accident, as spelling was a casual matter in those days. Claes' son, Nicholas Roosevelt, was a New York alderman, or member of the town council, from 1698 to 1701. During the 18th and 19th centuries, the Roosevelts continued to play a prominent role in the business and the civic government of New York. Thus, Theodore Roosevelt was born into a family with a long tradition of wealth, good works, and public service.

DIVIDED LOYALTIES

Roosevelt's father, Theodore Roosevelt, Sr., was a partner in the firm of Roosevelt and Son, which imported plate glass. He was sufficiently well off that he did not need to spend very much time at his office; instead, he devoted a great deal of his time and energy to charities and cultural institutions. He donated money that helped found the New York Orthopedic Hospital, the Metropolitan Museum of Art, and the American Museum of Natural History, all in New York City.

His wife, Martha Bulloch Roosevelt, or "Mittie," came from Georgia. Her Scottish, English, and Huguenot (French Protestant) ancestors had helped to colonize the South, and one of them had served as the first governor of Georgia during the Revolutionary War. Born and raised on a plantation, she was a traditional southern belle when she married Roosevelt in 1853. Indeed, she was so accustomed to Georgia ways that she found it difficult to set up house in New York without black slaves. Although she soon adjusted to northern life, she never lost her love of the South.

Young Theodore was born in the family home on East 20th Street on October 27, 1858. He had an older sister—

Anna, whose nickname was "Bamie"–but he was the first son and was named after his father. Later another boy, Elliott, and another girl, Corinne, were born. Theodore, whose own nickname was "Teedie," called them "Ellie" and "Conie."

Theodore's early childhood was touched by the sweeping tragedy of the Civil War, which broke out in 1861. The senior Roosevelt was a staunch Republican and supporter of President Lincoln. He backed the northern, or Union, cause. But his wife could not deny her sympathy for the South, which she still considered her home. Two of her brothers, Theodore's uncles, served in the southern, or Confederate, navy.

During the war, Mittie Bulloch Roosevelt gave food, clothing, and some money to the Confederate cause by means of secret Confederate agents in New York. At the same time, her husband was drafted into the Union army. As was the custom for many wealthy men of the time, Roosevelt paid another man to serve as his substitute in the army. Nevertheless, he helped the Union by working as a paymaster and touring army camps.

The war years were sometimes difficult for the Roosevelt household because of the opposing loyalties of Theodore's mother and father. But the future President had the advantage of hearing politics discussed from an early age – and of being encouraged to take an interest in the subject.

FROM SICKLY TO STRONG

People who knew the vigorous Theodore Roosevelt during his adult life would have been surprised to learn that he was a sickly, feeble child. He was thin, weak, and pale almost from birth, and during his boyhood he suffered terribly from asthma (a disease whose victims sometimes have great difficulty breathing). So severe were the breathing and choking problems connected with his asthma that young Theodore often had to sleep in a sitting position, propped up with pillows in bed or in a chair. He also had more colds, coughs, and other sicknesses than most children.

In addition to his physical weakness, Theodore also had poor eyesight. He discovered this one day while playing with other children, when he learned that they could read the words on a billboard a block away. "Not only was I unable to read the sign, but I could not even see the letters," he said later. Theodore's eyes were examined by a specialist, and from that time on he wore glasses.

Despite his puny physique and poor health, Theodore was a high-spirited and proud child. He keenly resented the teasing he sometimes received from stronger, more active boys. Sensing his son's unhappiness, Theodore's father offered a suggestion: through a rigorous program of physical training, he explained, Theodore could build up his muscles and make himself stronger. Theodore was excited about the idea and vowed to stick to his training program faithfully. So his father bought him the necessary weights and other equipment to set up a small gymnasium on the second floor of the Roosevelt home.

Although some of the exercises were difficult or boring, Theodore worked out in his gym with great persistence, almost never missing a day. He received guidance from experts in physical training at Wood's Gym in New York, where he sometimes went to work out. Progress was slow but sure. And before a year had passed, the once-scrawny Theodore had developed broader shoulders and muscular arms and legs. He could now run and jump to his heart's content.

Theodore's experience with his home gym was typical of the man he would become. He leaped at a chance to change something he did not like, and all his life he continued to believe that taking action was better than simply enduring an unpleasant situation. From his earliest years, he grew accustomed to thinking of himself as a man of action. His train-

A Very Respectable Family 9

ing program also demonstrated the qualities of determination and stubborn persistence that would accompany him throughout his life.

Becoming a Fighter

By age 11 or 12, Theodore had developed strength and muscular size unusual for his age. As he was soon to learn, however, strength cannot solve all problems — sometimes skill is needed, too. When he was about 13, Theodore suffered a humiliating experience. He was on a train bound for Moosehead Lake in Maine to recover in the country after a bad asthma attack. Two boys riding in the same part of the train started picking on him, making fun of his proper "little rich boy's" clothes, his eyeglasses, and his upper-class accent. Soon the bullying grew into a fight, and Theodore, despite his newfound muscles, got the worst of it.

Theodore was furious and embarrassed that he had not been able to fight back. He decided to add boxing lessons to his training program, so that he would be able to defend himself if he ever needed to do so again. His father bought a punching bag and boxing gloves for the second-floor gym. He also hired John Long, a one-time prize-fighter, to come to the house and train Theodore. Amateur boxing was to be part of Theodore's life for many years — until he had an accident while boxing in the White House.

TRIPS ABROAD

Because Theodore's father did not need to spend a great deal of time at his business, the family was able to take long trips. During the winter of 1869–1870, when Theodore was 11, the Roosevelts toured Europe. They spent Christmas in Rome, where Theodore was presented to Pope Pius IX, whose hand he politely kissed – even though the family followed the Dutch Reformed faith and not that of the Catholic Church.

At this time, Theodore was not yet as healthy and vigorous as he would be a year or two later. Because he was not very active, he found the trip rather dull. At one point, when he was feeling lonely, his mother showed him a photograph of Edith Kermit Carow, one of Corinne Roosevelt's playmates in New York. In the diary he kept of the trip, Theodore wrote that the sight of Edith's familiar face made him extremely homesick. Many years later, Theodore would marry the woman whose face had reminded him of home.

Three years later, during the winter of 1872–1873, the Roosevelts made another long trip. They returned to Europe, and this time they also went to Egypt, where they enjoyed a long, leisurely voyage up the Nile River in a sailboat. From Egypt, they went on to Palestine and visited the ancient cities of Jerusalem and Bethlehem.

After leaving the Holy Land, the Roosevelts went to Dresden, Germany. Theodore and two cousins spent several months there, living with a German family while studying French and German. They amused themselves by writing stories and essays, which they then read to each other at the meetings of a club they called the Dresden Literary American Society. One of the cousins later described Theodore at this time as "a very amusing boy but . . . he was very absent-minded. He always thought he could do things better than anyone else."

Theodore had a much better time on the second trip. For one thing, he was much healthier and more active. At Giza, in Egypt, for example, he was able to scramble to the top of the famous Pyramids – an awkward and difficult climb even for an adult. The other reason he had more fun on the second trip had to do with his love of natural history.

THE YOUNG NATURALIST

At that time, the sciences of biology and geology were sometimes grouped together and called natural history, the study of the earth and all forms of life upon it. People who studied natural history or made collections of specimens were called naturalists. Theodore became a naturalist at a young age.

When he was seven, he saw a dead seal laid out on a slab at the local fish market. The seal filled him with excitement because it reminded him of adventure stories in faraway places he had read about. He visited the fish market every day to look at the seal; he even made careful measurements of its size and wrote them down in a pocket notebook. Eventually, he was given the seal's skull, possibly through the kindness of an amused fish seller.

With this prize, Theodore and two cousins started an exhibit they called the Roosevelt Museum of Natural History. They kept collections of rocks, bones, dead mice, and other interesting items in a dresser drawer. But when their treasures were discovered by a maid, she angered Theodore by throwing away a litter of baby mice. The children then moved their museum to an out-of-the-way bookcase in a little-used hall, where the seal skull remained the exhibit's chief item. That skull was the first natural history specimen Theodore acquired; there would be many more over the next 50 years.

Theodore's father, who was one of the founders of the American Museum of Natural History in New York City, encouraged his son's interest in the subject. He was delighted when, at age nine, Theodore wrote a very intelligent essay called "The Natural History of Insects," based on many hours spent observing ants, bees, and other creatures. Thus, by the time the Roosevelts toured Egypt, Theodore had already been an enthusiastic amateur naturalist for several years.

Theodore enlivened the trip by learning the Latin names

of all the birds he saw and by making an impressive collection of stuffed Egyptian and European birds. To do so, he had to become a good hunter, so that he could shoot the birds without damaging their skins. He also had to master the art of taxidermy, or the preparation of stuffed skins. With the help of his father and some useful books, he learned to hunt and to prepare stuffed birds quite well.

When Theodore returned to New York from Dresden in 1873, he came to a new home. His father had built a new brownstone mansion on West 57th Street. Theodore settled into the new family home and took stock of himself. He was now 15 years old, in robust physical health, and quite determined upon a career in science. He wanted to be a professional naturalist.

EDUCATION

Theodore's delicate health as a very young child had prevented him from attending school. When his parents finally did send him to school, one run by a Professor McMullen near the Roosevelt home, he became ill and left the school after only a month or so. For the rest of his childhood, he studied at home.

Theodore's first teacher was an aunt, his mother's sister, Annie Bulloch, who taught him the basics of reading and writing. She also recounted tales of the South and the Confederacy, which gave her young student a love of history. A number of other private tutors followed. The Roosevelts even hired a teacher of taxidermy to encourage Theodore's natural history hobby.

Upon his return to New York in 1873, Theodore decided to enter Harvard College as the next step toward his goal of becoming a naturalist. To prepare for the college's difficult entrance examinations, Theodore started a period of intensive studying with tutor Arthur Hamilton Cutler. He passed the examinations in 1875.

Harvard Years

In 1876, Theodore set off for Cambridge, Massachusetts, to start his freshman year at Harvard. The four years he spent there were a blur of activity—not all of it related to the young man's schooling.

Theodore did fairly well in classwork, especially in German and the sciences. His interest in natural history continued to grow, and he studied hardest in courses that dealt with that subject. He was characterized by tremendous curiosity; indeed, he asked so many questions during one lecture that the exasperated professor burst out, "Now look here, Roosevelt, let me talk. I'm running this course!" Theodore also did well in history, philosophy, and rhetoric (the art of using language effectively in writing or speech-making). Blessed with a remarkable memory, Theodore was able to read dozens of books on a given subject and quote long passages from them perfectly many months later. But his performance in Greek and Latin, which were required studies at that time, was poor.

Theodore was unable to confine his attention to the subjects of his classes. He read hundreds of books on anything that interested him. At this time, one of these "extra" subjects was naval warfare. He had had many long conversations with his uncles, his mother's brothers, who had served as high-ranking officers in the Confederate navy during the Civil War. Their stories aroused his interest in the subject of war at sea, and he went on to read about ships and famous sea battles. Near the end of his college career, he prepared two chapters for a book he was writing about the naval battles that took place during the War of 1812.

Hudson Area Public Library
Hudson, Illinois 61748

War at sea was a subject of lifelong interest for Roosevelt, who began writing a book about the naval battles of the War of 1812 while he was still a student at Harvard. He loved stories of heroic victories won against overwhelming odds, as in the Battle of Lake Erie, shown here with the American forces on the right and the British on the left. (Library of Congress.)

In 1878, when Theodore was a sophomore at Harvard, his father died at the age of 46. Although he inherited $125,000 from his father's estate, Theodore began to wonder whether this would be enough money to support him throughout his life; naturalists, he knew, seldom had much income. These thoughts about money took on additional meaning when, that same year, Theodore fell in love.

A New Romance

Theodore had long been very fond of Edith Carow, the child-hood playmate of his sister Corinne. As teenagers, Theodore and Edith had been drawn together by a shared love of books and nature. But when Theodore left New York for Harvard, the distance between them—and his new interests—caused the two young people to drift apart.

Then, in October of 1878, Roosevelt visited the home of Richard Saltonstall, one of his classmates, and met the Saltonstalls' neighbors, the Lee family of Chestnut Hill, Massachusetts. Their teenage daughter, Alice Hathaway Lee, was a charming and intelligent gray-eyed blonde, and Theodore fell deeply in love with her. By Thanksgiving, Theodore had decided that he wanted to marry Alice, and he proposed to her in June. She took several months to make up her mind, but finally accepted his proposal on February 14, Valentine's Day, of 1880.

In the meantime, of course, Theodore had been completing his college studies. Always a whirlwind of energy, he was busy with much more than just his classes. He was vice-president of the college's Natural History Club, and an officer of two social and theatrical clubs. He founded a finance club and edited a journal called the *Advocate*. He also wrote papers and lectured for the Nuttall Ornithological Club, a bird-watchers' organization.

On top of all these activities, Theodore continued to practice the physical training program he had learned as a child, spending many hours in the college gym. He also continued to box. In fact, he was runner-up for the college lightweight boxing championship.

The boxing match in which Theodore lost the championship title received much attention. His opponent was C. S. Hanks, a larger man and a better boxer. The bout became quite bloody and rather brutal until, at one point, Hanks hit Theodore after the bell had rung to end the round. When the audience jeered at Hanks' poor sportsmanship, Theodore insisted upon explaining to the crowd that Hanks had not heard the bell. He then shook hands with Hanks, drawing cheers from the crowd for both combatants. Although Theodore never wavered in his lifelong admiration for strength and physical bravery, he believed equally strongly in good sportsmanship.

During his senior year, Theodore wrote a long paper called an honor's thesis. It was accepted by the honors committee, which meant that he was able to graduate *magna cum laude,* or "with high honors." He also was made a member of Phi Beta Kappa, the national honors society. In the spring of 1880, just a few months after the announcement of his engagement to Alice, Theodore's college years came to an end. He graduated 21st in a class of 177 students. Now it was time for young Mr. Roosevelt to begin his career.

Chapter 3

Politician and Cowboy

At the time of his graduation from Harvard, Roosevelt faced a difficult decision. He was now 22 years old, and for more than a decade he had dreamed of becoming a naturalist. But he wondered whether, as a scientist, he would be able to provide for himself and the wife and family he expected to have. Alice, his fiancee, and J. Laurence Laughlin, one of his professors, suggested that he should consider giving up natural history in favor of a more secure career in law. After much thought, Roosevelt decided that a legal career had possibilities. It could, he felt, lead to political or public service.

Roosevelt had always been interested in politics. He had heard thoughtful debates — sometimes heated ones — on political issues in his home as he was growing up. He had enjoyed talking about politics and world affairs with his teachers and uncles. During his freshman year at Harvard, he became active in politics by joining a torchlight parade and demonstration in support of Rutherford B. Hayes for President. So, he decided to turn his attention to law and politics as a career. First, however, he wanted to travel and relax a little after four years of studying. He also wanted to get married.

Following his graduation from Harvard, Theodore spent

the summer hunting with friends in the Midwest. In the fall, he returned to the East for his wedding. He and Alice were married on October 27, his birthday; he was 22, she was 19. The wedding and reception took place in Alice's home town of Chestnut Hill, Massachusetts. All of Roosevelt's family and friends were there—even Edith Carow, his sister's friend and his own former girlfriend.

The newlyweds had a two-week honeymoon at the Roosevelt family's country house in Oyster Bay, Long Island. Then they moved into the brownstone on West 57th Street with Roosevelt's mother, and Roosevelt set about starting his law career.

As a first step, Theodore enrolled in Columbia Law School. He also obtained some training in the law office of an uncle, Robert B. Roosevelt. But he found that the study of law did not interest him. He spent most of his first year in law school completing the book he had begun at Harvard. It was called *The Naval War of 1812: or, the History of the United States Navy During the Last War with Great Britain*, and it was published in 1882.

By the time his book was published, Roosevelt had dropped out of law school. He and Alice then took a trip to Europe, where they engaged in such strenuous athletic pursuits as mountain-climbing in Switzerland. Upon their return to New York, Roosevelt began to pursue his interest in political life. He joined a Republican club and, when friends chided him that politics was not a gentleman's activity, he replied that he wanted to be one of "the governing class."

FIRST POLITICAL OFFICE

In 1881, Roosevelt was asked to run for the office of representative to the New York State Assembly. As a member of the powerful Republican Party and of a wealthy and well-known

The Naval War of 1812

Roosevelt's book on the naval actions during the War of 1812 is still considered one of the most authoritative and enjoyable books on that subject. The War of 1812 was a hard-fought conflict that pitted the Americans against the British in many parts of the United States and Canada. Roosevelt rightly recognized the excellent performance of the Americans in several important sea battles. He described some crucial United States naval victories with excitement and accuracy.

America's first big victory in the war took place in August of 1812. It was the capture of the British warship *Guerrière* by the American frigate *Constitution* under the command of Captain Isaac Hull. The *Constitution* is probably the most famous American naval ship of all time. Launched in 1797, she saw service against French privateers, North African pirates in the Mediterranean Sea, and British gunboats in the War of 1812. It was during the engagement with the *Guerriere* that the *Constitution* received its nickname. The American sailors, seeing that the British shells could not penetrate the ship's sturdy oaken hull, dubbed her "Old Ironsides."

The great old ship eventually became un-seaworthy and was scheduled to be destroyed in 1828. But Oliver Wendell Holmes' poem "Old Ironsides" aroused the public to raise funds for the restoration and preservation of this historic vessel. The *Constitution* is now moored and open to visitors in Boston.

She has never been taken off the list of commissioned ships in the U.S. Navy.

The second great American naval victory occurred in September 1813 on Lake Erie, where a British squadron was patrolling the lakeshore to keep Americans from reaching British positions in Canada. Commodore Oliver Hazard Perry, with the help of his officers and men, hastily repaired and equipped a tiny fleet of one brig, six schooners, and one sloop. With this small force, he managed to destroy the entire British squadron.

A year later, a third major naval battle took place on Lake Champlain, between New York State and Vermont. The British had 11,000 men and 16 vessels; the Americans had only 1,500 men and 14 smaller vessels. Yet the American commander, Captain George Downie, cunningly maneuvered the British into a position where they could not bring their long guns to bear on the American ships. The British were soundly defeated, and the Battle of Lake Champlain marked the end of their attempts to invade New York.

Other naval skirmishes, on the Great Lakes and at sea, showed the United States to good advantage in a long, bitter war that did not end in clear victory for either side. With typical enthusiasm and positive thinking, Roosevelt focused attention on one part of the War of 1812, describing how smaller and weaker American forces were able to use skill and determination to defeat a larger and stronger enemy.

New York family, he had no difficulty getting elected. He took office in January of 1882; at age 23, he was the youngest member of the Assembly. His political career had begun.

Unlike many junior legislators, Roosevelt had no intention of sitting quietly by while his elders ran the show. He quickly became one of the most talkative and active assemblymen in the state capital of Albany. He was the leader of and spokesman for a group of Republicans who wanted to make changes and improvements in many laws and practices.

For example, Roosevelt and his colleagues felt that it was government's responsibility to regulate certain trades and industries in order to protect workers. They sponsored bills to eliminate the terrible conditions of the tenement workshops in New York City. These were ramshackle old houses in which workers, usually poor immigrants, lived and worked. On an inspection of one such workshop, Roosevelt saw an entire family rolling cigars in the single, vermin-infested room in which they all lived. This experience made him a firm opponent of unregulated business. Roosevelt and like-minded legislators succeeded in getting some bills passed that called for closer regulation of the tenement workshops.

Roosevelt and Machine Politics

Early in his political career, Roosevelt declared his opposition to "machine politics," the system in which elected legislators were completely under control of the political party to which they belonged. Politicians, especially young ones new to the world of politics, were expected to act and vote pretty much as they were instructed to do by their party.

As a staunch individualist and independent thinker, Roosevelt would have no part of such a system. Although he was a member of the Republican Party and agreed with its stand on many issues, he refused to be hampered in his think-

ing and actions by party directives. He argued so energeti-
cally against machine politics, and he upset the established
system so often, that he was soon nicknamed the "Cyclone
Assemblyman."

During Roosevelt's first year as an assemblyman, he an-
noyed the Republican machine by crossing party lines to take
the side of Governor Grover Cleveland, who was a Demo-
crat. He helped Cleveland pass legislation to reform the
method of electing aldermen in the state and the rules about
hiring government employees.

As a result of his support of Cleveland and of Democratic bills, the state's Republican Party bosses became un-
happy with the young legislator. Nevertheless, he was
re-elected in 1882 for the 1883 term, and he even served for
a short while as the minority leader in the Assembly, but the
party soon removed him from that powerful position.

When Roosevelt was re-elected in 1883 for the 1884 term,
he was named chairman of the New York delegation to the
Republican National Convention, which was to be held in
Chicago. As chairman, he prepared the New York delegation to vote for Senator George F. Edmunds of Vermont as
the Republican presidential candidate.

BIRTH AND DEATH IN THE FAMILY

Roosevelt's third year in the Assembly was notable for three
important events in his personal life. On February 12, 1884,
his first child, a daughter, was born. Roosevelt was thrilled
to have a child and looked forward eagerly to playing with
and teaching his new daughter.

Tragically, however, his beloved wife, Alice, died two
days later, on Valentine's Day, the fourth anniversary of their

engagement. She suffered from Bright's disease, a condition that combines high blood presure with a blood disorder, and the complications of childbirth proved fatal.

That Valentine's Day was an especially black one for Roosevelt. In another part of the house, his mother also died that day, of the deadly infectious disease typhoid fever. The 26-year-old Roosevelt was now alone with his baby daughter, whom he named Alice after her mother. In his deep grief, he wrote in his diary that he felt his own life was over.

Driven by his belief in duty and the value of hard work, Roosevelt continued to carry out his legislative responsibilities, leaving little Alice in the care of his sister, Anna. Even in politics, though, the year was a sad one. At the Republican National Convention, Edmunds failed to receive the presidential nomination. Instead, the convention nominated Senator James D. Blaine of Maine.

Supporting the Party's Choice

Because Roosevelt felt that Blaine was a corrupt and incompetent politician, he tried hard to prevent him from being nominated. After the nomination was settled, however, he eventually came out with an endorsement (a public statement of support) for Blaine. This action pleased the Republican machine, but Roosevelt was learning that no politician can please everyone.

When he finally endorsed Blaine, Roosevelt earned the scorn of a group of reform-minded Republicans who had refused to back Blaine. These renegade Republicans, who were called Mugwumps, gave their support to the Democratic candidate, Grover Cleveland. By failing to join the Mugwumps, some of whom were former colleagues in the New York State Assembly, Roosevelt drew criticism from newspapers and politicians who favored reform. But he stood firm. Although he continued to feel that Blaine was a poor choice, he said publicly that Blaine had been fairly nominated and should be supported by loyal Republicans as the party's choice.

Once the furor of the convention was over and his third term in the Assembly was drawing to a close, Roosevelt decided that he needed a change. No doubt he was still mourning his wife's death and found too many memories in the big, echoing house on 57th Street. Perhaps, too, he had found the fierce infighting of machine politics a bit distasteful. At any rate, he did not run for a fourth term. Instead, he decided to take a long break from home, from politics, and from the East Coast. Like many restless Americans before him, he went West.

HOME ON THE RANGE

Roosevelt had already traveled in the American West and learned to love its wide-open spaces, clear air, and rugged way of life. In September of 1883, during a visit to the Badlands region of the Dakota Territory, he had bought a partnership in the Chimney Butte Ranch for $50,000. Now, in the late summer of 1884, he returned to the Dakota Territory and purchased a new ranch, the Elkhorn, on the Little Missouri River.

At first, Roosevelt made a somewhat odd cattle rancher. His eyeglasses, eastern accent, good manners, and new clothes stood out glaringly among the shabby garments and western drawls of the other cowboys. He quickly gained a new nickname, "Four Eyes," and he was a constant source of merriment to the rough westerners who surrounded him. His first cattle roundup was long remembered by the cowhands. In-

In 1885, Roosevelt posed in an elaborate outfit of western rancher's gear for this photograph. During his two years in the West, he gained fame as a hunter and deputy sheriff, and he acquired a love of the outdoors that never left him. (Library of Congress.)

stead of bellowing out "Giddy-up!" or "Let's go!", Roosevelt urged the men to "Hasten forward quickly, there." The cowhands laughed until tear-tracks streaked their dusty faces.

But Roosevelt could ride and shoot, and he soon learned how to rope a steer, repair a fence, and do all the other tasks demanded of a rancher. His strength, honesty, and straightforward bluffness were qualities a cowboy could appreciate. They also admired his fighting skills, which were demonstrated when he knocked out a drunken cowboy who menaced him with two drawn guns.

Roosevelt gained local fame as a hunter, too, especially after one trip to the Big Horn Mountains. He and some friends were out hunting game on a mountainside when Roosevelt suddenly found himself face to face with a huge grizzly bear. He fired a single bullet and prepared to leap out of the way of the charging beast, but the charge didn't come. The bear dropped dead, killed with a perfect shot between the eyes. It weighed more than a thousand pounds, and Roosevelt treasured its skin for many years.

Before long, Roosevelt was regarded with pride as one of the territory's best men. In a small way, he returned to political life. He served for a time as deputy sheriff and even helped round up an outlaw band. He was an organizer and chairman of the Little Missouri Stockmen's Association, through which he encouraged the ranchers to cooperate with one another to get the best possible prices for their beef in the eastern markets.

Goodbye to the West

Roosevelt's western life was broken by frequent train trips to New York to visit his daughter and to conduct business. During one of these trips, in 1885, he ran into Edith Carow at his sister Corinne's house. He and Edith began to correspond and to see one another whenever Roosevelt was in New York. In November of that same year he proposed to her. She accepted. Because his first wife's death was still rather recent, however, they followed the custom of the time and made no public announcement of their engagement. Roosevelt returned to his ranch, where serious troubles awaited him.

The winter of 1885–1886 was one of the worst in western history. Severe snowstorms blanketed the Great Plains, killing as many as three-quarters of all the cattle in the region. Like other ranchers, Roosevelt lost many cattle and a considerable amount of money. This disaster, combined with his plans for a second marriage, made him decide that his ranching days were over.

Although Roosevelt was a rancher for only two years, he remembered them all his life. "Here the romance of my life began," he later wrote of his arrival in the West. "Whatever may happen I can thank God that I have lived and toiled with men. . . . I never would have been President if it had not been for my experiences in North Dakota."

The ranching years had been productive ones in many ways. Roosevelt had not only ridden the range, he had also written a number of books. One was a biography of Thomas Hart Benton, a Missouri senator and good friend of President Andrew Jackson during the early middle years of the 19th century. Roosevelt then wrote a book about Gouverneur Morris, a New York statesman of the Revolutionary era. His writings of this period also included several books about his western experiences: *Hunting Trip of a Ranchman* and *Ranch Life and the Hunting Trail*. In addition, he wrote a four-volume history of America's westward expansion, which was published between 1889 and 1896. It was called *The Winning of the West, 1769–1907.*

One other important result of Roosevelt's years in the West was the great increase in his love of nature and the outdoors. He had always had an amateur naturalist's interest in the natural world, but now he passionately appreciated its beauty and magnificence. He was to become an important conservationist, partly because of his exposure to the splendor of the western lands.

RETURN TO NEW YORK

In the fall of 1886, Roosevelt returned to New York City and his two-year-old daughter. He let his friends and associates in the Republican Party know that he was interested in returning to political life as well. His first effort, however, was not very successful. In November, he ran for mayor of New York against Abram S. Hewitt, the Democratic candidate. Because New York City had a Democratic majority, Hewitt won the election. Roosevelt placed third, after another candidate, economist Henry George.

The following month, Roosevelt had a happy celebration to help him forget his mayoral defeat. On December 2, 1886, he and Edith were married in London. The wedding took place in a famous cathedral, St. George's of Hanover Square. It was small and quiet; it was also rather dim, because the thick fog for which London is notorious had filled the church. Only the groom stood out clearly in the dimness, for he was wearning unconventional bright-orange gloves.

After a 15-week honeymoon tour of Europe, Roosevelt and his new wife settled down with little Alice in New York. From this time on, they made their home at the Roosevelt country estate, a large gabled mansion called Sagamore Hill on Oyster Bay, Long Island. Roosevelt turned his attention

Edith Kermit Carow became the second Mrs. Roosevelt in 1886. She and Roosevelt had known one another since early childhood. (Library of Congress.)

to writing, completing several of the books that he had begun during his ranching days.

In 1888, he campaigned in the Midwest for Benjamin Harrison, the Republican candidate for President. Harrison was elected and, when he took office in 1889, he appointed Roosevelt to a $3,500-a-year post as a member of the U.S. Civil Service Commission. When Grover Cleveland became President for the second time in 1893, he reconfirmed the appointment of his one-time supporter in the New York State Assembly, even though Roosevelt had supported Harrison's re-election campaign in 1892. Roosevelt served on the Commission for six years, until 1895.

The Civil Service Commission

Roosevelt's years on the Civil Service Commission were a useful preparation for a career in the federal government. The commission's purpose was to oversee the administration of civil service jobs. It was a huge and difficult task and, once again, Roosevelt found himself swimming against the tide of machine politics.

Civil service jobs are government positions—federal, state, or local—that are filled on the basis of merit and not by political appointment. At first, these jobs were filled through a system that was eventually called the "spoils system," from the phrase "To the victor belongs the spoils," which means that the winner gets the prizes. In the case of civil service, the prizes were jobs, and the winner of a campaign generally awarded them to friends, supporters, or people who had contributed money or other aid to the campaign. Every time someone new was elected to public office, all the people who had held jobs under the previous office-holder would be swept out of their offices and the jobs would be turned over to new people — usually members of the party machine or members of their families.

This system, also called patronage, was standard practice for many years. But as the country and the government became larger and more complex, the need grew for standards of skill and ability in government jobs. In addition, many people believed that replacing the entire staff of a government bureau or office every four or eight years was not a very efficient way to run things.

The question of patronage jobs came to a crisis about eight years before Roosevelt was appointed to the Civil Service Commission. In 1881, President James A. Garfield was assassinated by a man who was angry because he had failed to obtain a government patronage position. Congress then passed the Pendleton Act, which established the Civil Service Commission to administer standard examinations as part of the process of qualifying for a civil service job. The commission was designed to eliminate political patronage in the granting of most government jobs.

Naturally, many established job-holders and political interests resented the activities of the Civil Service Commission. But Roosevelt, ever the reformer, paid no attention to their outcries and steadfastly waged war against anyone who defended the spoils system. During his six years on the commission, the number of civil service jobs in the country doubled, and Roosevelt strove to ensure that every one of them was filled on the basis of merit. He was not completely successful, but he made notable strides. In his hands, the country's civil service system went from being a laughingstock to winning a large measure of public trust and respect.

CLEANING UP THE POLICE

Roosevelt's successes on the Civil Service Commission received much attention in his hometown, New York City. In 1895, Mayor William Strong, who wanted to make reforms in city government, invited Roosevelt to become president of the city's Police Board. The New York City Police Department was notorious for widespread corruption, and Roosevelt knew that reforming it would be a big job. But he accepted the challenge and withdrew from the Civil Service Commission to start his new duties.

At the time, New York's police department was plagued by patronage – the same problem Roosevelt had worked on to stamp out in the civil service. Many men were given jobs as policemen because they had friends in local political organizations. High-ranking jobs were often awarded to the man who could give the best gift to a local politician; in other words, jobs were sold. The belief that hiring and promotion should be based on merit or ability was not widely held.

Bribery was also widespread in the police force. Many policemen were more than willing to accept a bribe in exchange for looking the other way while a crime was committed. Even the many honest policemen were discouraged by the corruption around them. When he took on his new job, Roosevelt described the police department as "utterly demoralized" and riddled with "venality and blackmail."

In truth, Roosevelt had little real power as president of the Police Board. He did not outrank the high-level members of the police department. The changes he wanted to make had to come about through recommendations and negotiations, not direct orders. But Roosevelt knew that the high-ranking police officers were protected by powerful friends in the local Democratic and Republican machines, and he was aware that his recommendations and suggestions would not get far unless he was able to put some muscle behind them. He found that muscle in the newspapers.

The Yellow Press

During his years on the Civil Service Commission, Roosevelt had seen the power of the press. On many occasions, newspaper publicity about a corrupt individual or practice had brought about a public outcry for reform, which was soon followed by the reform itself. Roosevelt believed that the majority of people wanted their government and their police department to be honest and honorable. He felt that the best way he could accomplish his goal of reforming the corrupt police department was by using publicity—or the threat of publicity—to get his way.

The newspapers of New York City at that time were perfect for his purpose. Two papers were vying fiercely for readers. They were the *World*, owned by Joseph Pulitzer, and the *Journal*, owned by William Randolph Hearst. The cutthroat competition between these two papers led to an increase in the use of sensational items. Large, dramatic headlines, photographs with misleading captions, and other sensationalistic tricks of the newspaper trade became daily features of New York journalism during the rivalry between these two papers in the 1890s.

The competition between the *World* and the *Journal* extended even to the comic pages. A cartoonist for the *World* created a comic whose main character was a ragamuffin child dressed in yellow. This comic, called "The Yellow Kid," became so popular that the *Journal* lured the cartoonist away from the *World* with a raise in pay. Thereupon the *World* hired another artist to continue the comic. The cartoon wars were nicknamed "yellow journalism," and that phrase soon came to stand for the whole trend toward competitive, sensationalistic newspapers.

In their thirst for attention-grabbing headlines, the yellow newspapers were eager to print stories that exposed corruption in high places or criticized prominent people. These stories were read by thousands of people, and the outcry they raised was often heard even by people who did not read the sensational papers. Roosevelt knew that the yellow press would be more than willing to cooperate in his drive to clean up the police department, and that the people who read the papers would be on his side. He decided to make the newspapers his weapon against corruption.

Bribery and Blackmail

Roosevelt's first step was to confront the police chief, who was the strongest opponent of reform. Roosevelt obtained information about bribes that the chief had taken, and he threatened to tell the newspapers about the bribes unless the chief resigned. The threat was effective; the police chief resigned. Roosevelt was actually using his own form of blackmail to get what he wanted, but he believed that a little quiet blackmail was a suitable weapon for dealing with a scoundrel.

During his term as president of the Police Board, Roosevelt did not limit himself to sitting in an office or attending meetings. He believed, in this as in every other job he ever did, that it was necessary for him to get a first-hand look at what was going on and to be personally involved. He would wander around the city late at night, wrapped in a dark cloak and with a hat pulled low over his face, looking for policemen who were lazy, inefficient, or drunk. Sometimes he took reporters with him so that they could write scathing

This cartoon from 1895, just after Roosevelt became president of the New York City Police Board, was called "A Roosevelt to the Rescue." It shows the "Able Reformer" rolling up his sleeves to free New York from crooked politicians of both parties. (Library of Congress.)

articles about the offending policemen for the next day's papers.

One reporter who often accompanied Roosevelt on his nightly rambles was Jacob Riis, a Danish-born writer who fought passionately for social reforms. His book, *How the Other Half Lives*, had been published in 1890 and was widely read; it shocked middle- and upper-class Americans by calling attention to the miseries suffered by the urban poor. As a prominent journalist, Riis supported Roosevelt's reform movement and helped the reforms get plenty of publicity.

One of Roosevelt's reforms got attention from as far away as Europe. It involved the sale of liquor on Sundays. New York had a law, called the Sunday Excise Law, that strictly banned the sale of any liquor on Sunday. For many years, large numbers of people had ignored the law because it was felt to be old-fashioned and unnecessary. Despite the law, saloons and beer gardens would stay open on Sunday in all parts of the city.

Roosevelt, however, announced that the law must be enforced. He closed down saloons that opened on Sunday and issued fines to their owners. Although he drank little himself, Roosevelt did not object to liquor; he didn't even mind people drinking on Sunday. In fact, he thought that the Sunday Excise Law was a bad law. But, he felt, the law is the law, whether it is popular or not. "I do not deal with public sentiment," he said. "I deal with the law."

Closing down saloons might have been expected to make Roosevelt unpopular. But, on the contrary, it increased the people's respect for him. Articles in most American and some European newspapers praised his devotion to duty and the law. His name became synonymous with honesty and trust.

Not everyone liked Roosevelt, of course. New York City's Democratic political machine (called Tammany Hall at that time), the gangsters who controlled crime and vice in the city, the corrupt police officials who were in the pay of politicians and gangsters, and even some members of Roosevelt's own Republican Party opposed his reform movement. The politicians were angry because Roosevelt ignored political pressure. He set up a system of hiring and promotion by merit, which meant that politicians could no longer reward their supporters with police jobs. He also refused to allow even minor laws to be broken or bent to serve the interests of local politicians. Committeemen who owned saloons, for example, complained furiously to the political parties when their businesses were shut down on Sundays, but Roosevelt kept on with his work. Before long, the public admired and trusted him, and the honest members of the police force felt new enthusiasm and respect for their jobs.

FAMILY MATTERS

While he was serving on the Civil Service Commission and the Police Board, Roosevelt was also enjoying his new family. After their marriage, he and Edith had immediately brought little Alice to live with them at Sagamore Hill. Soon they began to have children of their own. Theodore Roosevelt, Jr., was born in 1887; Kermit Roosevelt was born in 1889, the year his father took up his post on the Civil Service Commission; Ethel Carow Roosevelt was born in 1891; and Archibald Bulloch Roosevelt was born in 1894, just before his father accepted the Police Board presidency. The house at Oyster Bay was a lively place, with the five young children and their friends and pets constantly romping through it.

In 1896, Roosevelt again became active in national politics. Still president of the Police Board, he took part in the Republican presidential race. He favored Thomas B. Reed of Maine, who was the Speaker of the House of Representatives, for the Republican presidential nomination. But when William McKinley won the nomination, Roosevelt campaigned wholeheartedly for the party's choice in the Midwest and the East.

At about this time, a friend mentioned to Roosevelt that his great popularity with the public and the press might make *him* a likely presidential candidate. "Don't you put such ideas into my head," Roosevelt retorted. "I must be wanting to be President. Every young man does. But I won't let myself think of it." It is likely, though, that he did think of it sometimes, because soon he eagerly accepted an opportunity to return to a position of national importance—one that he probably thought of as the next step in an ambitious career.

Chapter 4
A Republican Hero

After McKinley's election in 1896, Roosevelt asked the new President to find him a position in the federal government. Of course, Roosevelt did not want to be accused to seeking a patronage job—he asked to be given a position only if he were qualified for it. Because Roosevelt was well-liked by some powerful political friends, including Senator Henry Cabot Lodge of Massachusetts, McKinley agreed to see if there was a place for him in Washington.

Eventually, the President offered Roosevelt the post of assistant secretary of the Navy. Roosevelt accepted the $4,500-a-year job and took office in 1897 under Secretary of the Navy John D. Long. He was considered well qualified for the position by virtue of his proven honesty and administrative experience; in addition, he was the author of a well-known book on naval warfare.

AT THE HELM

Anyone who had read Roosevelt's book carefully could have predicted how he would act as assistant secretary of the Navy. In the preface to *The Naval War of 1812,* he pointed out the disastrous consequences of being unprepared for war. He argued in the book and in some of his later writings that the United States should always be strongly armed and ready for war, with an effective Army and Navy. This readiness, he felt, would prevent war from breaking out—and if it *did* break out, the better-prepared side would certainly be more successful.

Ever since his first boxing lesson, Roosevelt had been a firm believer that individuals should be ready and able to defend themselves, and he applied the same principle to countries. As soon as he had settled into his new office, he set about doing what he could to strengthen the Navy and make it ready for anything that might happen.

Roosevelt tackled his new duties with the same energy, zest, and eagerness to reform that he brought to all his activities. He reorganized the system for ranking and promoting naval officers much as he had reorganized the New York City Police Department. He urged the government to consider the military potential of airplanes and set up a panel to study the "flying machine." And he made innumerable recommendations and proposals, most of them aimed at increasing the size and strength of the Navy.

John Long, Roosevelt's superior in the Navy Department, was in poor health and was glad to turn over much of the day-to-day responsibility for running the department to his lively young assistant. At times, when Long was absent due to illness, Roosevelt functioned quite capably as acting secretary. But Long occasionally complained about Roosevelt's endless activity and his tendency to take matters into his own hands, without consulting his superiors.

"He is full of suggestions, many of which are of great value," Long said, "and his spirit and forceful habit is a good tonic; but the very devil seems to possess him—distributing ships, ordering ammunition which there is no means to move to places where there is no means to store it; sending messages to Congress for immediate legislation authorizing the enlistment of an unlimited number of seamen." Roosevelt's impatience—the "devil" Long spoke of—came from his passionate belief in the widely held theory that the United States was destined to play a greater part in world affairs.

Manifest Destiny

Since its founding, the United States had been growing and extending itself farther westward. By the early 19th century, most Americans shared the belief that the United States should eventually occupy the entire continent, bringing its unique form of government and society to the territories of the West.

In 1845, New York editor John L. O'Sullivan claimed that it was America's "manifest destiny to overspread the continent allotted by Providence for the free development of our yearly expanding millions." The phrase "manifest destiny" (manifest means "obvious" or "undeniable") came to be used for the feelings of national pride and expansionism that characterized the era. Manifest destiny was used to explain the addition of Texas to the Union, the claim against England for the Oregon Territory, the war against Mexico in 1846, and the purchase of Alaska from Russia in 1867. And many people, including Roosevelt, felt that America's destiny—and its opportunities to expand—need not be limited to the North American continent.

Critics of manifest destiny claimed that it was just another way of talking about greedy, old-fashioned empire-building. But Roosevelt and some other expansionists truly believed that the strong, prosperous, democratic United States had a responsibility to help other, less civilized nations—though that help may have looked like interference or even domination. Roosevelt's belief in the necessity of expanding America's influence was one reason why he wanted a strong Navy. At the time he took up his post in the Navy Department, he foresaw a coming conflict that would test the theory of manifest destiny.

WAR WITH SPAIN

The United States and Spain had crossed swords many times during the past century. The United States had not wanted other countries to have colonies in North America, but Spain had owned Florida and Mexico for a long time. Spain also owned Cuba, a fertile island in the Caribbean Sea only 90 miles south of Florida. In the 1890s, many Americans, including Roosevelt, felt that Spain had held on to Cuba too long. They thought the island should belong to the United States, which had many business interests there.

The Cuban people did not particularly want to belong to the United States. They did, however, want to be free of Spanish control. Starting around 1895, the Cubans began rebelling against their Spanish overlords in a series of uprisings. The rebels attacked and destroyed both Spanish and American property, hoping to drive the two nations into war with one another. Such a war, the rebels felt, might give Cuba a chance to declare its independence. General Valeriano Weyler, Spain's military commander on the island, reacted by treating the peasants of the Cuban countryside with dreadful brutality in an attempt to crush the rebellion.

Many newspapers in the United States leaped into the conflict. Stories of brave peasant rebels and cruel Spanish generals made colorful, exciting reading in the yellow press. William Randolph Hearst's New York paper, the *Journal,* called Weyler a butcher and urged the United States to take Cuba away from Spain for humanitarian reasons. Other papers joined the outcry, and many public leaders began to feel that an attack on the Spanish in Cuba was a good idea. Roosevelt described the Spanish hold on Cuba as "murderous oppression" and said many times that the United States had an obligation to take the island away from Spain.

Tension grew until relations between Spain and the

United States were at the breaking point. That point was reached in February of 1898. Hearst somehow obtained a copy of a private letter written by the Spanish ambassador to the United States. In this letter, the ambassador criticized President McKinley in unflattering terms. Hearst published the letter in the *Journal,* and the American public reacted with angry indignation. People cried out for war against Spain. Six days later, another incident enraged the Americans still further.

The Explosion of the *Maine*

The American battleship *Maine* was moored in the harbor of Havana, Cuba. It had been sent there to show the Spanish that the United States was ready to protect the lives and property of Americans in Cuba. Sadly, the *Maine* did not last long enough to carry out this task. On February 15, it blew up and sank in the harbor, killing more than 250 American crewmen.

An official investigation by the United States determined that the two explosions that destroyed the ship had been caused by a floating mine. Immediately, Spain was accused of the crime. American newspapers—especially the *World* and *Journal*—fanned the fires of pro-war feeling with the slogan "Remember the *Maine,* to hell with Spain!" Ironically, a second investigation, carried out many years later with more modern scientific techniques, showed that the explosions were caused by a fire in the ship's coal storage area that ignited the ammunition stores, not by a Spanish mine. In 1898, however, no American would have believed such an explanation for a moment.

Americans cried out for war: to free the Cubans from Spanish tyranny, to seize Cuba for the United States, or simply to avenge the *Maine.* President McKinley, however, be-

America was outraged by the explosion of the U.S. battleship Maine in Havana Harbor in 1898. Although a later investigation showed that the ship was not really destroyed by Spanish mines, the incident helped set off the Spanish-American War. (Library of Congress.)

lieved that war should be avoided if at all possible. Roosevelt became impatient with the President's attempts to keep the peace, and he said to friends that McKinley had "no more backbone than a chocolate eclair."

In the meantime, Roosevelt doubled his work on behalf of a strong Navy, because he felt that sea power would determine the outcome of the war. He wanted to put the Navy on full alert around the world. Without asking the advice or permission of his superiors, he sent a telegram to George Dewey, commodore of the U.S. fleet in the Pacific, telling him to attack the Philippine Islands as soon as war was declared. It is probably due to this telegram that the Spanish-American war extended into Asia as well as the Caribbean.

Even the peace-loving McKinley soon realized that war was inevitable. Although Spain might have been willing to withdraw from Cuba after prolonged negotiations, the public demanded war and the President knew that it was unwise to ignore the nationwide outcry. On April 11, he asked Congress to declare war.

A declaration of war was passed on April 25. But it carried a special clause, called the Teller Amendment, that had been added by congressmen who did not want the other nations of the world to think that the United States had made war on Spain simply to add Cuba to its own territory. The Teller Amendment declared that, in the event of a U.S. victory over Spain, the United States would not annex Cuba – that is, Cuba would not become a U.S. territory.

Roosevelt's Rough Riders

Roosevelt had never served in the armed forces, except for a stint in the New York National Guard from 1882 to 1885. He had received no military training, and he certainly had never seen any battle action. Yet, at age 39, he unhesitatingly resigned his position in the Navy Department less than two weeks after war was declared in order to volunteer for military service. "I had always felt," he said later, "that if there were a serious war I wanted to be in a position to explain to my children why I did take part in it, and not why I did not take part in it." By the time he volunteered for war duty, Roosevelt had six children; Quentin, the last of his children, had been born in 1897.

The secretary of war at the time was Russel A. Alger. He was Roosevelt's friend, and he shared Roosevelt's belief that war with Spain was necessary. After convincing Congress to authorize the formation of three volunteer regiments of cavalrymen, Alger invited Roosevelt to recruit and command one of the regiments. Roosevelt always held a high opinion of himself, but he was also realistic. He knew that, without a military background, he would not be the ideal commander—at least until he had gained a little experience in the field. So he suggested to Alger that command of the regiment be given to Colonel Leonard Wood.

Colonel Wood was a friend of both Alger and Roosevelt; indeed, he was Alger's doctor. Wood was an army surgeon who had won the Congressional Medal of Honor in recent battles against the Apache Indians in the West. Because he had plenty of military experience, Wood was given command of the regiment, and Roosevelt was made his lieutenant colonel.

Wood and Roosevelt selected a handful of seasoned veteran officers and put them in charge of obtaining the necessary equipment for the regiment, which was to be organized in San Antonio, Texas. That city made a good gathering point for two reasons: plenty of horses were available in Texas, and it was near the ports of the Gulf of Mexico, from which the troops could take a ship for Cuba.

Next, Alger sent telegrams to the governors of Arizona, New Mexico, Oklahoma, and the Indian Territory announcing the formation of the First U.S. Volunteer Cavalry Regiment and asking for 500 volunteers. He added that the volunteers should be "young, sound, good shots, and good riders." The telegram also listed Wood and Roosevelt as senior officers of the regiment.

Before long, the volunteers poured into San Antonio. Many of them were friends of Roosevelt, or men who had heard of him. Some were policemen from New York City and other eastern locations who respected him for his work on the Police Board. A few were gentlemen hunters and sportsmen. But the greatest number were cowboys from the West who had ridden the range with Roosevelt and were more than willing to follow him to Cuba. These rugged individuals soon earned the regiment its nickname: the Rough Riders.

The Cuban Adventure

The War Department decided that the First U.S. Volunteer Cavalry Regiment was to sail for Cuba not from San Antonio but from Tampa, Florida, which was much closer to Cuba. The men, their horses, and their equipment were quickly carried by troop train to Florida. There the docks swarmed with excited confusion. More than 17,000 men—regular Army troops, volunteers, and officers—were waiting to ship out for the scene of battle. Unfortunately, there were not enough ships to carry all the men and their horses and gear. Weapons, ammunition, and the most necessary supplies were loaded aboard the ships; everything else, including the horses of the Rough Riders, was left ashore.

The Rough Riders made the short voyage to Cuba in the ship *Yucatan*. They were landed a week's march away from

Santiago de Cuba and set off for that city through the dripping, rainy jungle. On the way, they had a few minor skirmishes. They successfully beat back a Spanish force that tried to ambush them at Las Guasimas on June 24. Wood was promoted on the spot to the rank of major general, and Roosevelt was made a full colonel and acting commander of the regiment. Six days later occurred the famous battle of San Juan Hill — and Roosevelt's leap to fame as the leader of the charge.

The Rough Riders lost 100 men — one-fifth of their total — during that battle. Over the following month, many more of them became ill with tropical fevers and diseases that severely weakened them. But the battle of San Juan Hill had broken the Spanish resistance, and U.S. naval forces destroyed the Spanish fleet off Cuba two days later. On July 17, when Santiago de Cuba formally surrendered, the 24,000 Spanish troops on the island also lay down their arms. With Cuba secure, Roosevelt insisted in August that his ailing troops be recalled to the United States.

The Rough Riders landed at Montauk Point on Long Island. Soon afterward, those who were well enough to walk were among the veterans of the Spanish-American War who marched down Broadway in New York City, rained upon by clouds of confetti and deafened by the cheers of a huge crowd. The New Yorkers gave an especially warm welcome to their hometown hero, Teddy Roosevelt, as he was now known to the newspapers. Then the First U.S. Volunteer Cavalry Regiment was formally mustered out of service (disbanded) on September 15.

Roosevelt's short but glorious military career was over. He always remembered it as one of the high points and great accomplishments of his life. "I would rather have led that charge," he said later, "and earned my colonelcy than served three terms in the United States Senate. It makes me feel as though I could now leave something to my children which will serve as an apology for my having existed." And he never forgot the wild exhilaration of his charge up the hill. "San Juan," he once said, "was the greatest day of my life."

End of the War

While still assistant secretary of the Navy, Roosevelt had arranged matters so that the United States would attack Spanish positions in the Pacific if war broke out in Cuba. Commodore Dewey followed Roosevelt's instructions and led his squadron into Manila, the capital of the Spanish colony of the Philippines, on May 1. He sank the Spanish fleet at anchor, beseiged the city, and captured it on August 13. The U.S. Navy had also captured Guam, a tiny Spanish island in mid-ocean that was useful as a fueling station. In addition, the Navy seized Wake Island, another potentially useful dot on the map that no one had previously claimed. Roosevelt's daring plan to carry the war into Asia had succeeded. When Dewey returned home, he was treated as a hero, promoted to the rank of admiral, and given the post of president of the Naval Board.

The Spanish-American War lasted only 10 weeks, but the peace negotiations took a bit longer. The United States honored the Teller Amendment and did not try to take control of Cuba, although some expansionists wished to do so. The United States did insist, however, on taking over Spain's claims to Guam, the Philippines, and Puerto Rico (another Caribbean Island that had been a Spanish colony for centuries). Having been outclassed and soundly defeated in battle, Spain was forced to agree. On December 10, 1898, representatives of the two nations signed the Treaty of Paris, which gave the United States three new territories.

Not everyone in the United States believed that it was right for America to annex these territories. Many prominent Americans protested loudly against the treaty; these included financier Andrew Carnegie and author Mark Twain. Critics of the annexation claimed that democracy by force was not true democracy, and that the people of the territories should be made independent and allowed to choose their own systems of government.

Roosevelt and others, however, believed that the United States had a duty—its manifest destiny—to bring American-style civilization and government to lands that had been oppressed by Spanish tyranny. In a more practical vein, people who favored the treaty pointed out that a secure base in the Philippines could be very advantageous to the United States. It could open the door to trade with the Far East, especially with China. This idea, which came to be called the Open Door Policy, carried the day. Although it faced a hard battle in the Senate, the Treaty of Paris was finally approved.

American naval bases and other operations were quickly set up on Puerto Rico and Guam. Even Cuba leased some land to the United States to be used for military bases. But subduing the Philippines to American control was not so easy. The Filipino people were happy to see the last of Spain, but they had no wish to become the colony of yet another overseas power. Led by Emilio Aguinaldo, the Filipinos carried out a bloody war of independence for four years. Finally, though, they gave way to the superior force of the United States. The Philippines became a U.S. territory and the site of an important naval base. In 1945, after World War II, the Philippines were granted independence. Puerto Rico remains a commonwealth of the United States, and Guam is still an overseas U.S. territory.

GOVERNOR OF NEW YORK

The hero of San Juan Hill had no difficulty with the next step of his political career. Just two weeks after the Rough Riders were disbanded, the Republican Party of New York State nominated him as its candidate in the 1898 race for governor. The Republicans were smarting from a recent scandal involving crooked contracts for work on state canals. A popular war hero who was also known as a dedicated reformer, they felt, would be just the thing to improve their image with the public. But here again, as in his three years in the New York State Assembly, Roosevelt had to deal with machine politics.

The leader of the New York Republican Party was Thomas Collier Platt, a state senator. Called Boss Platt because he was the undisputed party chief, he disliked Roosevelt and disapproved of his record as an independent-minded reformer. But the Republicans needed Roosevelt just then, so Boss Platt made up his mind to offer the nomination to Roosevelt—if Roosevelt would agree to follow the party line after he was elected. Roosevelt told Platt's assistant that, as governor, he would certainly confer with party officials (meaning Platt), but that he would have to follow his own judgment. Reluctantly, Platt accepted that statement as the best he could get, and Roosevelt won the nomination.

Many reform-minded voters were dismayed that Roosevelt appeared to have made peace with Boss Platt, and the candidate received some sharp criticism. Although he campaigned vigorously, making speeches in cities and towns all over the state, Roosevelt did not win by the landslide that his backers in the party had expected. Instead, he won by a slender margin of only 18,000 votes. However close the contest, though, Roosevelt had won. He was sworn in as the governor of New York in early 1899, taking up his duties in the state capital of Albany.

During his two years as governor, Roosevelt carried out his promise to discuss problems and issues with Platt. In reality, however, he almost always ignored Platt's advice and instructions and did what he believed to be necessary or right. Using a combination of persuasion and blackmail (his old trick of threatening to call in the newspapers), he got the state legislature to pass a number of reform laws. Among these were laws limiting the number of hours women and children could work and laws to better regulate tenement workshops (sometimes called sweatshops). He also got schoolteachers' salaries raised and started a state conservation program.

The Ford Franchise Act

Governor Roosevelt had many conflicts with Boss Platt, but the biggest battle concerned state taxes on corporations. John Ford, a state senator from New York City, introduced a bill that would tax corporate franchises (special licenses that protected railroad companies, electric companies, and other businesses from competition). Platt and his followers, who were supported by business interests, were horrified, because the Ford Franchise Act would cost these businesses millions of dollars in profits. To their dismay, the act passed the legislature. All that remained was for the governor to sign it into law.

The Ford Franchise Act was Roosevelt's first effort to curb the power of big business in America; it would not be his last. He believed that many businesses and corporations had grown so large and wealthy that they thought themselves above the law, breaking regulations and bribing politicians without fear of punishment. He also believed that big business did not serve the best interests of the American people and should be governed more closely.

But when the time came to sign the Ford Franchise Act, Roosevelt held off. He approved of its intention, but he felt it was actually a bit too strong. So he allowed Boss Platt to suggest a modified version, which ultimately became law. Platt was not much appeased by this gesture, however, because Roosevelt had made it clear that the revised act had to contain most of the features of the original. Passage of the act was considered a significant reform and a triumph of strategy for Roosevelt.

Near the end of his first two-year term as governor, Roosevelt was extremely well liked by the press and the people of the state. His honesty and hard work were respected, and he took pains to communicate often with the public through articles and speeches. The *World,* always a Democratic newspaper, admitted that "the controlling purpose and general course of his administration have been high and good." To most people, Roosevelt was simply the best governor New York had ever had. It was clear that he could be re-elected easily for a second term. But Boss Platt had other ideas.

Chapter 5

From Vice-President to President

Boss Platt definitely did not want Roosevelt in Albany for another term as governor, introducing reforms and bustling about upsetting Platt's schemes. But he knew that Roosevelt was so popular that he could not fail to be elected. The only chance to get rid of him was to find him a job somewhere else.

Fortunately, 1900 was a presidential election year. McKinley was sure to run again as the Republican candidate, but his Vice-President, Garrett Hobart, had died in office in 1899. McKinley had not yet found a running mate. So Platt decided that Roosevelt would make a good Vice-President— and he would be in Washington, not in Albany. Platt put the party machinery in motion, planning to have Roosevelt nominated at the national convention.

THE RELUCTANT VICE-PRESIDENT

Roosevelt was alarmed. He did not want to be Vice-President. Like many people, he thought of the vice-presidency as a boring, do-nothing job. In fact, he and some of his friends set to work to *prevent* the nomination. At the same time, however, Platt began urging westerners, who were fiercely loyal to the one-time cowboy Roosevelt, to support the nomination. They liked the idea and did not realize that it was part of a plot to put their hero out of the way.

Enthusiasm increased, and it soon became clear that Roosevelt would be nominated. He could always refuse to accept the nomination, of course, but that would be difficult to explain and might ruin his political career for good. Finally, Senator Lodge of Massachusetts, who had helped Roosevelt get his Navy Department post, advised him to accept the nomination. Lodge knew that Roosevelt dreamed of becoming President. The vice-presidency, he said, might prove to be a stepping-stone to the White House. Lodge was right—but he did not know how soon his words would come true, or under what tragic circumstances.

Roosevelt and McKinley

McKinley was not delighted to have the ambitious and aggressive Roosevelt as his running mate, but he made no public objection. When the Republican National Convention rolled around, McKinley was nominated as the presidential candidate, and Roosevelt made a speech seconding the nomination. Next, Roosevelt was nominated as the vice-presidential candidate and the convention was asked to vote on the nomination. Roosevelt thought it would be ungentlemanly to vote for himself, so he did not vote at all. He therefore received 925 of the possible 926 votes.

Not all of the Republicans were pleased with their vice-presidential candidate. One senator, Mark Hanna of Ohio, protested that there would be only one life between "that madman" and the White House. His words, too, were to take on a tragic echo all too soon. In the meantime, Hanna agreed to act as the manager of the McKinley-Roosevelt campaign because of his friendship for McKinley.

Senator Mark Hanna of Ohio managed the McKinley-Roosevelt campaign in 1900—but he did it for McKinley. He did not like or respect Roosevelt and called him a "madman" and a "cowboy." (Library of Congress.)

This political cartoon shows Roosevelt, wearing his trademark
hat and mounted on a toy horse, being introduced to McKinley, who is dressed as a little boy. "Willie" McKinley's father is
identified as "The Trusts," or corporations, that Roosevelt
would later attack; Senator Hanna, in the background, is
dressed as a nursemaid. "Teddy" is ironically described as
"very timid and retiring." (Library of Congress.)

William Jennings Bryan, the Democratic opponent of McKinley in 1900, was a skilled and famous orator who nevertheless failed to become President. He disapproved of the ideas about manifest destiny that Roosevelt shared with many other Republicans; to Bryan, interfering in the affairs of other nations was empire-building. (Library of Congress.)

At that time, it was the custom for incumbents — people who already held office and were running for re-election — not to campaign for themselves. Only those trying to be elected to new posts campaigned. So the burden of the McKinley-Roosevelt campaign fell on Roosevelt. He stumped around the country (the expression comes from the early practice of speech-making from atop a tree stump) drumming up support for the Republican team. Before the election in November, he made 673 speeches in 567 cities and towns in 24 states.

The Democratic candidate, William Jennings Bryan, accused the McKinley administration of being empire-builders. He pointed to the Spanish-American War and the annexation of the Philippines as evidence of a dangerous warlike tendency in the Republican Party. But because the United States had been victorious in that war and was enjoying a period of prosperity and good feeling, the people did not respond to Bryan's criticisms. The Republicans won the national election by a comfortable margin.

McKinley was sworn in for his second term on March 4, 1901. He planned to devote his energies during the coming term to developing trade treaties with other nations of the world. There were no pressing internal disturbances and no threats of war or other crises abroad. Everyone expected a calm, peaceful four years.

Roosevelt, on the other hand, found it boring. After his inauguration as Vice-President, he spent much time away from Washington and complained that he had little to do. "I do not think the President wants me to take any part in affairs or give him advice," he told friends. "The vice-presidency ought to be abolished." He decided to occupy his spare time by planning hunting trips and by resuming his study of the law, which he had interrupted 20 years before.

Assassination

On September 6, 1901, Roosevelt was having lunch with members of the Vermont Fish and Game League at Isle La Motte in Lake Champlain. McKinley was not far away, in Buffalo, New York, attending a large cultural and commercial fair called the Pan-American Exhibition. He had just made a speech in support of his pet project: new trade ventures between the United States and other countries. Among the well-wishers who crowded around to shake his hand at the end of the speech was a man named Leon Czolgosz. As McKinley held out his hand, Czolgosz shot the President.

McKinley was not killed, only badly wounded. After he was taken to a nearby house, his aides sent a telegram summoning Roosevelt. The Vice-President hurried to Buffalo, where doctors told him and the nation's newspapers that the President would recover. Roosevelt waited in Buffalo for several days. Then, seeing that McKinley appeared to be regaining strength, he left for a family vacation at Camp Tahawus in the Adirondack Mountains of New York State.

A few days later, on September 13, Roosevelt was eating lunch on the shore of Lake Tear-of-the-Clouds. A panting messenger ran up and gasped that the President was dying. Roosevelt immediately set off on a 10-mile hike to the closest road, where he climbed into a horse-drawn buggy for a 40-mile ride to the nearest railroad station. As soon as he reached the station – at sunrise on September 14 – a special train rushed him to Buffalo.

Roosevelt was too late. McKinley was dead when he arrived. In the room next to the one where the President's body lay, U.S. District Court Judge John R. Hazel swore Theodore Roosevelt into office as the 26th President of the United States. At age 42, Roosevelt was the youngest man ever to become President. He was holding the office of which he had dreamed, but the occasion was not one of celebration. "It is a dreadful thing," he wrote later, "to come into the presidency this way."

ROOSEVELT IN THE WHITE HOUSE

People who had not wanted to see Roosevelt become Vice-President were shocked to think of him in the White House. Senator Hanna, his former campaign manager, who had always disapproved of him, is said to have exclaimed, "Now look! That damned cowboy is President of the United States!"

Most Americans, however, were confident that their new President—despite his youth—would do a good job. The newspaper headlines coined a new nickname for him: TR. Roosevelt was the first President to be called by his initials. Since then, the practice has been used for others, notably FDR (Franklin Delano Roosevelt), JFK (John Fitzgerald Kennedy), and LBJ (Lyndon Baines Johnson). TR made no secret of the fact that he hoped to be elected in his own right in 1904.

The first order of business for the new President was for Roosevelt and his family to settle into the White House. When the six children and their puppies, snakes, and ponies moved in, they brought a breath of fresh air to the somewhat stodgy President's residence. They and their friends—soon nicknamed the White House Gang—frequently cavorted wildly around the executive mansion, once going so far as to plan a mock attack that Roosevelt halted by means of an official message through the War Department. He often entered into the children's games.

Roosevelt also continued the strenuous games and sports that he loved. While governor of New York, he had astonished his aides by wrestling with a champion middleweight wrestler twice a week. Now he took up boxing again and invited sparring partners to the White House regularly until a blow from a young military assistant caused him to lose the sight of one eye. Although Roosevelt told no one of the loss for many years, he did stop boxing. Instead, he studied the Japanese martial art of jiujitsu, a form of which is popular today as judo, and was one of the first Americans to become proficient in an Oriental martial art.

Roosevelt also played polo and continued to ride, fish, hunt, and hike as often as he could make time for these activities. He played tennis on the White House lawn so often that his partners in the game were referred to as the "Tennis Cabinet." In addition, he loved swimming across the Potomac River, even in winter when it was clogged with floating ice. Nor was his love of natural history forgotten. When he could snatch a moment, he read about or observed animals and birds. He also read histories, biographies, poetry, and the popular novels of Sir Walter Scott and Charles Dickens. He explained his love of reading as a form of refreshment, saying, "I find it a great comfort to like all kinds of books, and to be able to get half an hour or an hour's complete rest and complete detachment from the fighting of the moment."

Edith Roosevelt calmly took up her responsibilities as First Lady in addition to the task of mothering six very active children. She was an efficient organizer and kept the household running smoothly. She also remodeled the White House, at a cost of $475,000, for greater efficiency and elegance. (It was during Roosevelt's presidency, in fact, that the name White House began appearing on official stationery. The building had been informally called the White House ever since it was painted white after being burned by the British during the War of 1812, but its official name before 1901 was the President's House.)

The Cabinet

Roosevelt did not discharge any of the Cabinet members who had begun their service under McKinley. There were eight of them: John Hay, secretary of state; Lyman J. Gage, secretary of the treasury; Elihu Root, secretary of war; Philander Knox, attorney general; John Long, Roosevelt's former boss, secretary of the Navy; Charles Smith, postmaster general; Ethan Hitchcock, secretary of the interior; and James Wilson, secretary of agriculture.

Of the eight, only Wilson remained in his Cabinet post for Roosevelt's entire administration. The other posts changed hands—some of them several times—as Cabinet members shifted responsibilities among themselves or left the Cabinet for other duties. All in all, there were 29 Cabinet members during Roosevelt's administration. He created a new Cabinet position, the secretary of commerce and labor, in 1903. He filled this post first with George Cortelyou, his personal secretary, and in later years with Oscar Straus, the first Jewish Cabinet member.

Roosevelt's Square Deal

Roosevelt did not have a formal policy or plan when he became President. Instead, his handling of national affairs was based upon a group of ideas that became known as the Square Deal. The four sides of the Square Deal were: solving social problems through reform; passing new laws to regulate big business; controlling the growing railroad industry; and conserving the country's environment and natural resources. Thus, Roosevelt approached the presidency as he had approached every other job in his life. He was not content to drift comfortably along but was only satisfied when he identified problems and tackled them head-on.

THE TRUST-BUSTER

Roosevelt's first annual message to Congress was delivered in December of 1901, just three months after he became President. It set forth several pieces of the Square Deal philosophy. One item mentioned in this first speech was conservation. Roosevelt, who would later be called the Great Conservationist, announced that he would change America's way of dealing with its public lands. But most of the speech was devoted to a plan of action that would continue through his presidency. This program earned him still another nickname: the Trust-Buster.

Trusts (also called holding companies) were large corporations that owned or controlled many other companies that might otherwise compete with the parent company. In this way, a trust enabled one large company or group of companies to prevent competition, keep prices for its goods high, and obtain a monopoly—that is, to be the sole provider of that particular good or service.

Some of America's most prominent millionaire businessmen, such as financier J. P. Morgan and oil magnate John D. Rockefeller, headed giant trusts. These company officials, sometimes called "captains of industry," were confident that their holding companies could not be toppled. The companies had been cleverly designed to outwit the laws against monopolies and trusts, such as the Sherman Anti-Trust Act of 1890. The holding company was believed to be a legal method of getting around the act. Big businessmen were therefore startled when they read Roosevelt's first speech in the newspapers.

"The captains of industry," the new President said, ". . . have on the whole done great good to our people. Without them the material development of which we are so justly proud could never have taken place. . . . Yet it is also true that there are real and great evils. . . . There is a widespread conviction in the minds of the American people that the great corporations known as trusts are in certain of their features and tendencies hurtful to the general welfare."

Morgan, Rockefeller, and other "captains of industry" were forced to sit up and take notice of this brash new voice in Washington when, in February of 1902, Roosevelt ordered his attorney general to file a lawsuit to dissolve the Northern Securities Company. This was one of the nation's largest holding companies. It controlled all railroad traffic between Chicago and the Pacific Northwest, and it ruthlessly eliminated any competition that might have brought rates down. The suit was settled in favor of the government, and the Supreme Court upheld the decision in 1904. Roosevelt, who believed that the farmers and laborers of the country needed a champion to protect them against abuse by big businesses, had begun his career as a trust-buster.

Other Domestic Affairs

In 1902, Roosevelt took the first of the many conservation steps he was to take as President. He signed the Reclamation Act, which called for dams and other projects to use the water resources of the West as effectively as possible. Work done under this act brought water into dry areas and relieved flooding in other regions. Roosevelt's name was attached to the largest project carried out under the act, the Roosevelt Dam in Arizona. It used the waters of the Salt River to turn a barren desert into exceptionally productive farmland.

Also in 1902, Roosevelt became involved in a labor dispute in Pennsylvania. In May, 150,000 coal miners went on strike against the mine owners. The miners wanted higher pay, shorter hours, and recognition of their union. The owners, who included J. P. Morgan and railroad millionaire George F. Baer, refused to deal with the strikers. The mines remained idle until October, during which time the owners steadfastly refused to negotiate and the jobless miners grew more desperate. Communities were suffering, too, as the shortage of fuel caused schools and hospitals to close. Matters seemed at a standstill.

Finally, Roosevelt took a drastic step. For the first time in American history, he caused the government to become involved in an industrial dispute. He felt that it was the government's right and duty to represent the American people in a labor problem that threatened the general welfare. He threatened to seize the mines and have them operated by the national guard if the two sides could not settle their dispute.

Although the mine owners were furious at Roosevelt's interference in what they believed to be a private corporate affair, he did succeed in persuading the owners and miners to put their grievances before a panel of judges called arbitrators. The arbitrators settled the strike largely in favor of the miners. Since that time, many strikes have been settled by arbitration panels.

During the rest of his administration, Roosevelt tried hard to maintain a fair balance between the needs and interests of the working class and the rights of private property owners like the mine owners. His background as a reformer made him sympathetic to the complaints of poor people and laborers, but he also believed strongly that the law—including the legal rights of corporations—should be upheld. He lashed out against the leaders of violent or illegal labor strikes, saying that these men were just as much "undesirable citizens" as a wealthy railroad executive who had cheated on his taxes.

FOREIGN AFFAIRS

Roosevelt handled foreign affairs with his own special blend of firmness and diplomacy. His philosophy was summed up by a West African proverb that he often quoted: "Speak softly

*During the strike of Pennsylvania coal miners in 1902, miners'
wives searched the dumps for scraps of coal to heat their
homes and cook their meals. Roosevelt took the drastic step of
threatening to take over the mines if the strike was not settled.*
(Library of Congress.)

and carry a big stick, and you will go far." To Roosevelt, this
saying meant: "Don't brag or bluster, but show that you are
prepared to fight if need be." It suited his lifelong belief that
strength and fighting skills were important for individuals and
for nations. So, in international relations, he was always tactful, polite, and soft-spoken—but he also demonstrated his
readiness to use the Army and Navy quickly and decisively.
This policy came to be called Big Stick Diplomacy, after
Roosevelt's favorite proverb.

One chance to exercise his diplomatic skills came in
1902, soon after Roosevelt became President. The South
American nation of Venezuela had fallen deeply in debt to

other countries, and now it refused to repay money that had been loaned to it by England, Germany, and Italy. These nations sent gunboats to blockade the harbors of Venezuela. It began to look as though one or more of the European nations might even try to seize control of Venezuela.

At this point, Roosevelt stepped in. He politely offered to serve as a go-between and help the countries resolve their difficulty. Although he spoke quite softly, the European countries knew that he also had a big stick—the U.S. Navy—ready to steam southward at his command to prevent any takeover of Venezuela. After the European countries agreed to accept his help, Roosevelt persuaded all four nations to submit their case to the International Court of Justice at The Hague, in the Netherlands. They did so, and the court ordered Venezuela to begin repaying the loans in 1907.

The incident was a diplomatic victory for Roosevelt, as many people felt that he had prevented a nasty war. His handling of the negotiations was so tactful and intelligent that the emperor of Germany, who had begun by resenting the interference of the upstart American, ended by becoming a warm admirer of Roosevelt.

In 1903, Roosevelt again used his diplomatic skills, to settle a long-standing disagreement between the United States and England. The exact boundary of the Alaskan Territory's panhandle—the strip of land that stretches south from Alaska along the western edge of Canada—had been in dispute since 1825. The matter was considered unimportant by both the United States and England, however, until gold was found in the region in the 1890s. Suddenly, the two nations began to argue over who owned what. Roosevelt suggested an arbitration panel of six members, three each from the United States and England. The suggestion was accepted, the panel settled the conflicting claims through a series of compromises and trade-offs, and the matter was settled peacefully.

THE PANAMA CANAL

By far the biggest decision of Roosevelt's early years in the White House was the go-ahead to build the Panama Canal — a waterway that cuts right across Central America to connect the Atlantic and Pacific oceans. To get from one ocean to the other, ships had always had to travel all the way down to the southern tip of South America, through the treacherous Straits of Magellan, and all the way up the other side of the continent. A canal through Central America would save enormous amounts of time and fuel.

Always a believer in the importance of sea power, Roosevelt felt that the nation that controlled a canal between the two oceans would be a mighty force in the world. He also recognized that the Far Eastern lands around the Pacific, which were considered remote and barbaric by most Americans and Europeans, were destined to play a great part in international economics and politics of the future. As one of the first Americans to foresee the importance of the Pacific region, Roosevelt urged his countrymen to enact trade and defense treaties with the Far East. The canal would help.

The Panama Canal already had a long history. As early as the 16th century, the Spanish had dreamed of cutting a channel across the isthmus (narrow land) of Central America. But such a task was impossible before the development of modern machinery, explosives, and engineering skills. In the 19th century, a French engineer, Ferdinand de Lesseps, had succeeded in building the Suez Canal in Egypt; it connected the Mediterranean Sea and the Indian Ocean. De Lesseps, backed by a French company, took on the challenge of the Panama Canal in 1878. After the French received permission from the South American country of Colombia, which owned Panama, the work began. By 1887, however, uncontrollable tropical diseases and engineering setbacks had bankrupted the French

Panama Canal Facts

One of the greatest achievements of Roosevelt's presidency was the start of construction of the Panama Canal, the waterway that was to connect the Atlantic and Pacific oceans and thereby revolutionize shipping and trade for the whole world. The building of the Panama Canal was the biggest single engineering job the world had ever seen. The French had tried to do it; they failed when their money ran out and tropical diseases killed huge numbers of their workers. Under Roosevelt, however, the Americans succeeded in driving a path through jungles, mountains, and fever-ridden swamps.

The Panama Canal:

- saves 8,000 miles of a sea journey from the East Coast to the West Coast of the United States.
- shortens a trip from Europe to Australia by 2,000 miles.
- is located in one of the world's wettest climates, with an annual rainfall of about 160 inches.
- was first planned by the Spanish conquistadores in the 16th century.
- is 40.27 miles long from coast to coast.
- is 300 feet across at its widest point.
- was originally to be built in Nicaragua.
- cost the United States payments of $40 million to France, $10 million to Panama, and yearly payments to Panama of $250,000 or more—in addition to the actual cost of building the canal.

- cost about $337 million to build.
- required the labors of up to 40,000 men at a time for more than 10 years to complete.
- handles between 30 and 40 ships each day, from luxury cruise liners to tramp steamers, battleships, and oil tankers; each vessel takes from six to eight hours to make the passage.
- was opened to traffic on August 15, 1914—just in time for World War I.
- was given to Panama in 1979 (effective in the year 2000) by President James Carter.

company. At this point, the United States began to take an interest in the project.

Not all nations were eager to see the United States gain such a powerful advantage. England, for one, objected to the idea of the United States taking over the canal project. One of Roosevelt's first acts as President was to sign a treaty with England pledging that the United States would keep the canal open to ships of all nations in return for England's pledge not to interfere. The next step was to buy out the French company's concession, or lease, in the Canal Zone; a price of $40 million was agreed upon. All that remained was to obtain Colombia's permission to proceed. This would require a suitable payment.

Gunboat Diplomacy

Colombia turned down the American offer. At that, Roosevelt instructed his administration to investigate the possibility of making a canal through Nicaragua instead of through the

The building of the Panama Canal was plagued with problems and engineering challenges. Here, cranes are used to free a steam shovel from the debris of a landslide. (Library of Congress.)

Panama section of Colombia. This horrified the French company, which would not receive the $40 million if the United States did not take up its concession in Panama. In desperation, the French, led by an engineer named Philippe Bunau-Varilla, planned a revolution that would declare Panama free of Colombia.

Up to this point, Roosevelt had been speaking softly. Now it was time to use the big stick. Once the French had told him of their plans, he sent a U.S. gunboat, the *Nashville*, to cruise the waters near Panama. Roosevelt explained that the purpose of the ship was to prevent any other world powers from getting involved in the struggle between Colombia and Panama, but in reality its purpose was to keep Colombian troops from reaching Panama to put down the "revolution."

Roosevelt's gunboat diplomacy, as it was later called, succeeded in both purposes. "I took Panama," he once said, and added "after Bunau-Varilla handed it to me on a silver platter." While Colombia fumed that Roosevelt had interfered in its internal affairs, the Republic of Panama declared itself independent. The United States gave official diplomatic recognition to the new nation. A few days later, in November of 1903, Panama turned over to the United States complete control of the Panama Canal Zone, a 10-mile-wide strip across the isthmus. The American canal project was under way.

Engineering and Epidemics

The building of the canal took 10 years, from 1904 to 1914. Success was due to the efforts of many thousands of men who worked on the canal, but to three men in particular. John F. Stevens designed the canal, including the complex system of massive locks and dams that allows ships to pass across the isthmus well above sea level. Colonel William C. Gorgas was

George Washington Goethals

John F. Stevens is remembered as the man who designed the Panama Canal, but George Washington Goethals is honored today as the man who got it built.

Goethals was born in Brooklyn, New York, in 1858. He attended the U.S. Military Academy at West Point and joined the Army Corps of Engineers after graduating. For 27 years, he worked on harbor and canal projects for the army and also taught engineering at West Point.

When Theodore Roosevelt called Goethals to the White House in 1907, the President told him that he had been chosen as chairman and chief engineer of the Panama Canal project. A few months later, Roosevelt signed a special order giving Goethals full authority to govern everything and everyone in the Canal Zone. "Now," Goethals told Roosevelt with satisfaction, "I have both feet on the ground and I'll build the canal."

Goethals succeeded. When the canal was opened to traffic in 1914, President Woodrow Wilson named Goethals the first governor of the Canal Zone. Other honors included a medal from the National Geographic Society, a promotion to the rank of major, and the thanks of Congress for distinguished service. He retired from his post in 1917, but was recalled to duty and asked to serve until World War I had ended. He then returned to New York City and opened his own engineering company.

Goethals died in 1928. Two of the many memorials to him are a gigantic monument on the Pacific coast of the Canal Zone and the Goethals Bridge in New York City.

Roosevelt's trip of inspection to Panama made him the first American President to leave the country while in office. He enjoyed the trip immensely and was, as he says here, "De-e-lighted!" with the progress that had been made. A tiny bear, which had become a Roosevelt trademark, peers through his binoculars. (Library of Congress.)

an Army doctor who introduced new health and sanitation practices to the tropics; he wiped out the deadly disease yellow fever in the area by 1906, and he reduced the disease malaria by 90 percent. Without his contribution, the canal could not have been built—or not without a horrifying cost in human lives. George Washington Goethals was an Army engineer who took over the project in 1907 and, with skill and determination, saw it through.

A fourth man also played a special part in the building of the canal. He was President Roosevelt, who was proud of the canal and rightly believed that he had made possible "the greatest engineering feat of the age." He was so enthusiastic about it that he broke the custom that called for Presidents to remain in the country during their administrations. He went to Panama to inspect the work in person and to encourage and congratulate the workers, and he enjoyed himself immensely. Photographs taken during his inspection show him with his shirt-sleeves rolled up, knee-deep in mud, wielding a shovel among the grinning diggers. He was the first President to leave the United States during his term of office.

Chapter 6
The Second Term

As the election of 1904 approached, Roosevelt had reason to feel pleased with his performance as President. He had taken action to achieve several goals that were very important to him—building the Panama Canal, opening the war on trusts and holding companies, and starting a nationwide conservation program. He had also settled a serious strike and several international disputes.

Roosevelt hoped that the people of the United States were pleased with his performance, too. For three years, he had been troubled by the knowledge that he had not been elected President; he had come to the presidency only through McKinley's death. He desperately wanted to prove to himself and the world that he was now the people's choice for President. To do so, he would have to win the election of 1904. He decided to break yet another presidential custom, that of not campaigning as an incumbent office-holder. He was the first President to campaign vigorously for his own re-election.

CAMPAIGN OF 1904

Roosevelt's first task was to win the Republican presidential nomination. Because he was so popular, he had only one serious rival within the Republican Party. That rival was Senator Mark Hanna of Ohio, who had opposed Roosevelt from the start. In late 1903, a "dump Roosevelt" movement began to form as Republicans who disapproved of Roosevelt gathered support for Hanna. But Hanna died in early 1904. By the time the Republicans met in Chicago in June for their national convention, Roosevelt was assured of the nomination.

After Roosevelt was nominated unanimously, the Republicans chose Charles W. Fairbanks, a senator from Indiana, as his running mate. They also agreed on a party platform, or set of issues and plans. This platform called for increased foreign trade, a strong Navy and merchant marine (commercial shipping fleet), and continued use of Roosevelt's Big Stick principle.

The Election of 1904

The Democratic candidates were Alton B. Parker for President and Henry G. Davis for Vice-President. Parker was a judge from New York. Davis, a former senator from West Virginia, was 81 years old and the oldest person ever to be nominated for national office. The Democrats' platform called for independence for the Philippines, statehood for the western territories, and the idea that the United States should stay out of other nations' affairs.

Roosevelt and Parker agreed on many issues. They both wanted to make trusts less powerful and to increase trade. Also, they both believed in the rights of workers and consumers. The biggest point of difference between the two candidates concerned how the United States should behave toward other countries. Roosevelt felt that the United States, now a large and powerful nation, should do good around the world—by force, if necessary. Parker condemned this notion as arrogant imperialism (empire-building) and felt that the United States should mind its own business. The campaign, therefore, centered on this issue.

The personalities of the two candidates also shaped the campaign. Roosevelt was colorful, outspoken, and popular; Parker was colorless, quiet, and not very well known outside his home state of New York. In November, the voters stood solidly behind Roosevelt. He received 7,238,834 popular votes and 336 electoral votes. Parker received 5,084,401 popular votes and 140 electoral votes. Roosevelt had won by the largest majority of any presidential candidate up to that time.

After his election, Roosevelt vowed publicly that he would not run again in 1908. He did so because, by the time his new term ended in early 1909, he would have been President for more than seven years. It was understood that no President should be elected more than twice; in other words, no President would serve more than eight years, or two terms. But Roosevelt had not been elected to his first three years in office. Therefore, it was possible that he could serve two full elected terms in addition to those three years, which would give him more than 11 years in office. To silence critics who complained that 11 years as President would give him too much power, Roosevelt agreed to regard his first three years in office as a first term. He promised not to seek re-election, but was later to regret this promise.

FATHER AND PRESIDENT

Roosevelt was inaugurated on March 4, 1905. His inaugural speech made it clear that he still believed strongly that America must take its rightful place as a powerful world leader. "We have become a great nation, forced by the fact of its greatness into relations with the other nations of the earth," he said, "and we must behave as beseems a people with such responsibilities. Toward all nations, great and small, our attitude must be one of cordial and sincere friendship. . . . But jus-

*Roosevelt, Edith, and their five children posed for this picture
in 1907, during his second term. Alice, Roosevelt's daughter by
his first wife, had been married the year before.* (Library of
Congress.)

tice and generosity in a nation, as in an individual, count most
when shown not by the weak but by the strong."

The years between 1905 and 1909 were busy and productive ones for Roosevelt the President. They were also busy
ones for Roosevelt the family man. His oldest child, Alice,
made her debut (her formal entry into adult society, signalled
by an elaborate party) in 1902, at the age of 18. She was as

energetic and forthright as her father, and she quickly became very popular with the public. Many of her escapades and outspoken remarks found their way into the newspapers, which called her Princess Alice. Once, when a friend remarked to Roosevelt that his daughter was not very ladylike, the President laughed and said, "I can do one of two things. I can be President of the United States, or I can control Alice. I cannot possibly do both."

In 1906, early in Roosevelt's second term, Alice was married in the East Room of the White House to Nicholas Longworth, a congressman from Ohio. Longworth later became Speaker of the House of Representatives. He died in 1931, but Alice Roosevelt Longworth stayed on in Washington for many years, until she died at the age of 96. She became a famous, witty hostess and was sometimes called "Washington's other monument." After her marriage, the White House was a bit quieter—but the other five children continued to keep things lively for the President.

Anti-Trust Activities

The war on monopolies, trusts, and holding companies that Roosevelt had carried on during his first three years in office continued during the second term. Roosevelt had nothing against large corporations, he frequently pointed out. What he objected to was not their size, but the wrongdoings of which they were guilty. One after the other, he brought lawsuits against the railroad, beef, sugar, steel, oil, and tobacco monopolies, forcing them to follow the letter of each law governing corporations. In all, he brought to trial 25 cases against trusts.

At the same time, Roosevelt was taking other actions to regulate and improve business. He persuaded Congress to pass two acts, called the Hepburn and Elkins acts, to control the railroad industry. One act prevented the railroads from setting their rates at artificially high levels; the other gave the government's Interstate Commerce Commission the power to regulate railroad rates.

In 1906, Roosevelt turned his attention to laws that would safeguard the health and welfare of consumers. Still a reformer, Roosevelt believed that unsafe or unsanitary working conditions and impure consumer products should not be permitted. At his urging, Congress passed the Pure Food and Drug Act to regulate the purity of ingredients in foods and medicines, as well as the conditions under which they could be manufactured. This act has been updated several times; it is supervised today by the Food and Drug Administration in Washington.

During the early years of the 19th century, hundreds of books and articles were published that exposed illegal, wretched, or unhealthy conditions in industry and among the poor. Roosevelt termed the authors of these sensational writings "muckrakers," because they stirred up so much unpleasant material. But as a reformer, he found much in their work to attract his attention and sympathy.

One of the most sincere and talented of the so-called muckrakers was Upton Sinclair. In 1906, he published a best-selling novel called *The Jungle* that painted a horrifying picture of danger and filth in the meat-packing industry. Roosevelt read the book and ordered an investigation of the nation's meat packers. That report described conditions as "sickening." Soon afterward, Roosevelt had Congress pass the Meat Inspection Act to regulate sanitary and safety conditions in the nation's stockyards and packinghouses. It was signed into law the day after the Pure Food and Drug Act.

Roosevelt's second term also included a financial crisis.

In October of 1907, a New York bank called the Knickerbocker Trust went bankrupt. In a chain reaction, the failure of this large bank caused the failure of a dozen other banks, some railroads, and other businesses across the nation. The New York Stock Exchange dropped sharply and a financial panic started. Some people blamed Roosevelt's war on trusts for the panic. Roosevelt, however, blamed poor management of big corporations for the slump. To help restore a stable economy, he held off bringing an anti-trust suit against the U.S. Steel Company and invested federal funds in some banks that were in danger of collapsing. The nation began to recover from the Panic of 1907 in early 1908.

Roosevelt's Record on Race Relations

Several incidents during Roosevelt's second term involved race relations. He disapproved of racial discrimination on moral grounds, and he also believed that black Americans should have more opportunity to participate in the government of their country. Early in his political career, Roosevelt had met with Booker T. Washington, a well-known black scientist and teacher, to talk about appointing more blacks to government positions. Later, in October of 1901, just weeks after becoming President, Washington became the first black American to have an official dinner with a President when Roosevelt invited him to dinner at the White House. Thereafter, Roosevelt tried to appoint qualified black people to some political offices, but his efforts were thwarted by politicians, especially in the South, who did not approve of blacks participating in government.

Roosevelt's record on race relations was not always good, however. A tragedy took place in Texas in August of 1906 that turned many black people against him. When a group

of armed men attacked some private houses and stores near
Fort Brown, an Army post at Brownsville, one homeowner
was killed. Black soldiers at Fort Brown were immediately
blamed for the crime, although there was never any evidence
to connect them with it.

The Brownsville Raid, as it was called, drew national
attention, most of which was extremely hostile to the black
soldiers. Roosevelt felt he had to do something; possibly because he may have believed that at least some blacks might
have been involved in the incident. At any rate, he ordered
dishonorable discharges for 167 black soldiers at Fort Brown.
In 1972, 66 years later, the Army reopened the case. When
an investigation showed that there had been no proof of any
wrongdoing by the black men, the Army formally changed
the dishonorable discharges to honorable ones.

The Great Conservationist

During his second term, Roosevelt continued the conservation efforts he had begun during his first three years in office.
Guided by Gifford Pinchot, who held the office of chief forester to America's public lands, the President developed a new
philosophy of conservation for the country.

Before Roosevelt's time, private industries were allowed
to develop lands owned by the government whenever possible. Ranchers were allowed to graze their herds on public
acres; foresters were allowed to make huge profits cutting
down the trees of public timberlands; and corporations grew
rich by exploiting the oil and minerals found on government
property. In addition, few Americans felt a need to protect,
or conserve, the resources or beauty of the country. Most
people did not yet realize that natural resources were limited
and should not be wasted. Nor did people understand the frag-
ile nature of the environment and the need to safeguard it.

Roosevelt helped change all that, but he was not completely modern in his thinking about environmental issues. For example, he allowed industrial development of some public lands to continue – but he initiated laws to limit or govern such development, and he forced the developers to pay taxes that went to help safeguard the land. He tried to share with Americans his strong belief that the land was a treasure to be protected and used with care. In his annual message to Congress in 1907, Roosevelt told the people, "To waste, to destroy, our natural resources, to skin and exhaust the land instead of using it so as to increase its usefulness, will result in undermining in the days of our children the very prosperity which we ought by right to hand down to them amplified and developed."

In 1903, Roosevelt had appointed a public lands commission to identify areas of government property that needed protection. Then, in 1907, he formed a similar commission for inland waterways (rivers, lakes, and streams). During his years in office, he set aside 125 million acres of national forest, 68 million acres of coal lands, and 2,500 water-power sites to be protected from development. In addition, he promoted the use of conservation techniques for forestry, such as planting young trees to replace the harvested ones.

Roosevelt established the country's first wildlife refuge (Pelican Island, Florida), and he named the first national monument (Devil's Tower, Wyoming). He went on to create 50 more wildlife refuges and to name 15 more national monuments. Also, the number of national parks doubled during his administration – new parks included Arizona's Grand Canyon and Petrified Forest, Oregon's Crater Lake, Washington's Olympic Mountains Park, Utah's Zion Park, Colorado's Mesa Verde, and South Dakota's Wind Cave.

Perhaps Roosevelt's most long-lasting achievement as a conservationist came in 1908, when he called the state governors and senior Democratic and Republican officials to a three-day conference at the White House. The subject of the conference was how to use and protect natural resources. By the end of the meeting, Roosevelt's persuasive skills had won many of the governors over to his point of view. They agreed to the formation of a National Conservation Commission; Roosevelt appointed Pinchot to head the commission. Soon afterward, 41 of the 47 states in the Union (Oklahoma had become a state in 1907) formed their own state-level conservation commissions.

FOREIGN AFFAIRS

Roosevelt was also active in foreign affairs during his second term. The building of the Panama Canal continued, of course, to his great pride. In the aftermath of the Spanish-American War, the United States took responsibility for supervising the foreign relations of Cuba, protecting the new island nation from other countries, although Cuba never became a U.S. territory. The United States also became involved in the affairs of another Caribbean nation, the island of Santo Domingo (which is divided between the present-day nations of Haiti and the Dominican Republic).

In late 1904, Santo Domingo had the same problem that had troubled Venezuela several years earlier: it could not pay its debts to other nations. Several European countries began to demand repayment, and Roosevelt feared a repetition of the Venezuelan confrontation, with armed forces arriving in Santo Domingo from Europe. The idea that Europeans might move their armies or navies to an island close to the United States was unacceptable to Roosevelt and most Americans. They felt that the power struggles and military disputes of

Europe had no place in the New World, and they disliked the thought that a European nation might acquire a foothold near the United States. This way of thinking had been shaped more than 80 years before in a speech made by President James Monroe in 1823. The message he sent to the world in that speech came to be called the Monroe Doctrine.

The Monroe Doctrine

The Monroe Doctrine was a political philosophy and policy that set forth America's complete separation from the European powers of the Old World. Under the Monroe Doctrine, the New World nations of North and South America were recognized as being fundamentally different from the nations of the Old World. American nations were (for the most part) republics; Old World nations were (again, for the most part) monarchies.

The Monroe Doctrine also declared that North and South America were off limits for colonization or invasion by European powers. And it went on to say that if a European nation *did* attempt to colonize, invade, or in some other way interfere with a nation in the New World, the United States would regard it as an act of war. The Monroe Doctrine, therefore, set up the United States as the protector of the entire Western Hemisphere. The United States was willing—even eager—to take on this responsibility in order to keep the powerful European nations at a safe distance. Born less than 60 years after the American Revolution, the Monroe Doctrine gave the United States a chance to grow without worrying about rivals or enemies at its doorstep.

Today, the Monroe Doctrine no longer shapes America's foreign policy. Two world wars and a vastly more complicated system of international trade and communications have shown that no nation or hemisphere can remain isolated from the rest of the world, and one country's dictating the rights of other nations—even when done as "protection"—is no longer accepted quite so readily. But in 1904, the Monroe Doctrine was very much alive.

The Roosevelt Corollary

The Monroe Doctrine offered Roosevelt a guideline for dealing with the problem of Santo Domingo. It was clear to the President that if the island's financial situation did not improve, the European nations to which Santo Domingo owed money might invade the island or try to exercise their influence there. Because this was an outcome that he wanted to avoid, he decided to add something to the Monroe Doctrine. Instead of waiting for a European nation to invade Santo Domingo, and then regarding the invasion as a hostile act under the Monroe Doctrine, Roosevelt wanted to prevent the invasion in the first place. He came up with the Roosevelt Corollary to the Monroe Doctrine (a corollary is a consequence or result of something that has gone before).

The Roosevelt Corollary was set forth in the President's messages to Congress in 1904 and 1905. He stated that if a nation in the Western Hemisphere failed to repay a debt, or if it mistreated foreign subjects who lived there, the United States could intervene and set matters right—thus preventing any other nation from doing so. The effect of the Roosevelt Corollary was to make the United States into a sort of international police force for the entire Western Hemisphere. If any New World nation was unable to keep order within its borders, the United States would do so, "however reluctantly," as Roosevelt put it.

The first action under the Roosevelt Corollary was to take over Santo Domingo's finances. Roosevelt appointed a

U.S. official to keep track of the island's income from taxes and customs duties and to begin a repayment program for its debts. Santo Domingo agreed to this supervision although, in truth, the small and weak country had little choice. Not everyone agreed with Roosevelt's actions, though. The Senate failed to confirm his treaty with Santo Domingo for two years, but the work of managing the island's accounts went on regardless.

The Peacemaker

After his successful management of the crises in Venezuela and Santo Domingo, Roosevelt decided to take a hand in another, more serious, international dispute. Russia and Japan were at war over some territories on the mainland of Asia that both countries claimed, even though these territories were technically part of China. Roosevelt and some other world leaders recognized that the Russo-Japanese War, which appeared to center around a few seaports and railways in faraway Chinese Manchuria, in reality threatened to ignite a world war because various European nations were allied by treaty to Russia or Japan. With the hope of preventing the war in Manchuria from spreading to other nations, Roosevelt offered to try to get Russia and Japan to agree to peace terms.

His efforts were successful. By 1905, the second year of the war, Japan had performed better on the battlefield, but its army and other resources were almost exhausted. Although Russia had fared poorly in combat, it had plenty of soldiers in reserve but wanted to end the useless, expensive conflict. Roosevelt invited representatives of both nations to Portsmouth, New Hampshire. There he prevailed upon them to accept a treaty that he helped write. The Treaty of Portsmouth was signed on September 5, 1905, bringing the Russo-Japanese War to an end.

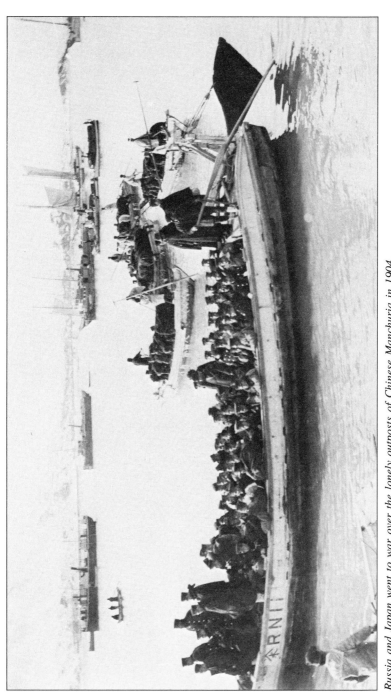

Russia and Japan went to war over the lonely outposts of Chinese Manchuria in 1904. Roosevelt's efforts to end the war earned him a Nobel Peace Prize. (Library of Congress.)

The New Power In The East

The war between Russia and Japan in 1904–1905 was significant to international politics because it marked Japan's emergence as a world power. It was the first time that the island nation, which was just coming out of a centuries-long period of isolation, engaged in war with a western nation. It also marked Japan's entry into the modern era.

Before the 20th century, Japan was very much like the feudal states of Europe during the Middle Ages (from about 500 to 1500 A.D.), with a powerful warrior class that lived by age-old customs. In the years immediately before the outbreak of war with Russia, however, Japan began to modernize its army, its educational system, its communications with the outside world, and its way of life. By attacking Russia, Japan announced to the world that it was now part of the international scene.

A decade earlier, Japan had fought a war with China over ownership of the Korean peninsula. Japan won a stunning victory in this war, but the western countries—the European nations and the United States—did not wish to see Japan become too powerful. At that time, the western countries were accustomed to dictating or influencing international policy in many parts of the world. They forced Japan to give up some of the territory it had won in the war against China. The Japanese especially hated giving up the city of Port Arthur, a deep-water port on the Chinese coast near Korea. They decided to try to get Port Arthur back as soon as possible.

Russia, however, also had designs on Port Arthur. At this time, Russia had not yet expanded to the full size of the present-day Soviet Union. The Russians were advancing toward the Pacific through Siberia and Asia. They had established a port at Vladivostok on the Sea of Japan, but it was far north of Port Arthur and was frozen for part of each year. Port Arthur, the Russians felt, was just the year-round seaport they needed on the Pacific.

Russia seized Port Arthur in 1898. The Chinese were too weak to protest, but the Japanese were furious. The northeastern part of China, where Port Arthur lay, was called Manchuria. Because this region had long been under Japanese influence, the Japanese felt that if any foreign power were going to control Port Arthur, it should be Japan. The Japanese immediately began building up their navy and army for an assault on Russia, one of the largest and strongest empires in the world.

Japan attacked the Russian forces in Manchuria in 1904. The Japanese navy won a number of important sea battles using such modern weapons as torpedoes and mines. Once the Russian navy was no longer a serious threat, Port Arthur was beseiged by the Japanese army, and the war became a test of endurance.

Both Russia and Japan poured men and

supplies into the wastelands of Manchuria, and the victories and defeats on each side were about evenly matched. Then the Russian defense of Port Arthur finally gave way, after which the Japanese inflicted terrible losses on the Russians in a great battle near Mukden, the capital of the province of Manchuria. In a bitter third blow to Russia, Japanese Admiral Togo wiped out the rest of the Russian fleet, which had hurried around the world from the Baltic Sea to attack Japan.

At this point, the Russians had used less than one-tenth of their total land force of nearly a million soldiers, while the Japanese had poured their entire armed force into the war and were growing desperately short of men and supplies. But Russia's remaining army was far away in Europe, and its entire fleet had been destroyed. In addition, the tsar (emperor) and Russian military leaders began to wonder how long they should go on fighting against an army that appeared fearless, highly disciplined, and absolutely determined to win. To make matters worse for the Russians, unrest in other parts of Russia meant that fewer resources were available to carry on the war in Manchuria. Neither side wanted to proceed, and neither side wanted to give up. Matters seemed to be at a stalemate — until Teddy Roosevelt offered to act as peacemaker.

The Treaty of Portsmouth, signed in the New Hampshire city on September 5, 1905, recognized that Japan had been the clear vic-

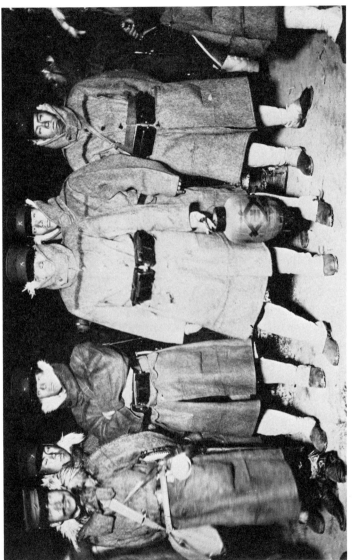

One of the most significant events of Roosevelt's presidency was the emergence of Japan—with a growing army of dedicated soldiers like these—as a major military power of the modern world. Roosevelt foresaw the growing international role of Japan and other nations of the Far East. (Library of Congress.)

tor in the Russo-Japanese War. It gave Japan
control of Port Arthur and much of Manchuria
under a lease from China. It also gave Japan
the southern part of Russia's Sakhalin Island,
which is north of Japan; Russia had seized
the island from Japan in 1875. The treaty
called for Russia to evacuate its troops from
Manchuria and recognize Japan's influence in
Korea.

Roosevelt's treaty ended the Russo-
Japanese War and was rightly regarded as a
triumph of diplomacy. Unfortunately, however, Japan was not satisfied with the results
of the treaty and grew increasingly militaristic
and aggressive. The Japanese seized outright
control of Korea in 1910, invaded Manchuria
in 1931, invaded southern China in 1937,
seized much of Southeast Asia as World War
II broke out in Europe, and finally attacked
the United States at Pearl Harbor in 1941.

The following year, Roosevelt was awarded the Nobel
Peace Prize in recognition of his contribution to ending the
war. He was the first American to receive the prize. When
he accepted it in person in 1910, Roosevelt included in his
acceptance speech a suggestion that the nations of the world
should unite in an international organization to promote peace,
prevent war, and settle disputes. This idea became a reality—
the League of Nations, forerunner to today's United Nations—
under President Woodrow Wilson a few years later. Roosevelt
used the Nobel Prize money, which amounted to $36,735, to
set up a fund to pay for research and projects to promote

The Nobel Peace Prize

Every year, five Nobel prizes are awarded, one each for physics, chemistry, medicine, literature, and peace. The cash prizes are paid from a fund that was set up by Alfred Nobel, a Swedish industrialist who invented dynamite and other explosives. The winners of the prizes are determined by committees from four Swedish and Norwegian academies of the arts and sciences.

The peace prize is awarded to the person who, or organization that, in the opinion of the committees, has done the most during the year to further the progress of peace and understanding among the nations and peoples of the world. In some years, the committees cannot agree, and no peace prize is awarded. And some of the awards have been controversial—for example, Adolph Hitler opposed the award of the 1935 peace prize to Carl von Ossietzky, a German who founded the Peace Society and tried to combat the rise of the Nazis. Hitler refused to allow Germans to accept any of the Nobel awards during his reign.

For the most part, however, the Nobel peace prize has gone to people whose contributions to the welfare of the world are unquestioned: Albert Schweitzer, who devoted his life to medical service in Africa; Martin Luther King, Jr., a leader of the civil rights movement in the United States; Dag Hammerskjold, who was secretary-general of the United Nations; and Mother Teresa, who has

served as a medical missionary in India. In
1906, Theodore Roosevelt joined the list of
distinguished people who have worked for
peace.

peace. Later, when the United States entered World War I,
he used the money from the fund to help war victims.

An Earthquake and an Agreement

One of the most serious and costly natural disasters in American history occurred during Roosevelt's presidency. On April 18, 1906, an earthquake rocked the West Coast from Los Angeles all the way north to Oregon. The earthquake was most severe in San Francisco and other cities near San Francisco Bay. About 700 people were killed outright, but worse was to come. A fire started in San Francisco right after the earthquake, probably caused by overturned oil lamps. It raged through the city, destroying many whole blocks of buildings, and did approximately $400 million worth of damage.

As San Franciscans began the long task of rebuilding their city, Roosevelt became involved in another racial controversy. Hundreds of laborers from China, Korea, and especially Japan were brought to San Francisco to work on construction projects. Trouble arose when the children of these workers were forced to attend segregated schools (schools that were separate from those for white children). Japan was angered by this treatment and claimed that it was a violation of an 1894 treaty between Japan and the United States.

Because Japan had become very warlike and aggressive in the years around the turn of the century, Roosevelt wanted

The people of San Francisco had to rebuild their city from rubble and ruin after a devastating earthquake in 1906. The inrush of Oriental construction laborers to the city got Roosevelt involved in an uproar over school segregation. He settled it by inviting school officials to the White House. (Library of Congress.)

to avoid a confrontation. In addition, he did not believe that segregated schools were necessary or desirable. He sent for members of the San Francisco School Board. When they arrived at the White House, he persuaded them to allow the Oriental children to attend the city's white schools.

The issue of the segregated schools was only part of a growing problem between whites and Japanese in California. Since the middle of the 19th century, Japanese immigrants had been arriving in California in large numbers. Some white Californians began to feel that these Oriental newcomers were occupying too many jobs and buying too much property in the state. In order to stop the unrest and hostility between the races, Roosevelt made a private deal—called the Gentleman's Agreement because it was never confirmed in a written treaty—with Japanese officials in Tokyo. Under the Gentleman's Agreement, Japan agreed to let fewer of its people emigrate to the United States. In return, Roosevelt promised not to pass any laws that would limit or entirely prevent Japanese immigration.

The Navy Goes Around the World

One event of Roosevelt's second term is considered a major achievement of his career. His first book had been about the U.S. Navy, and his first federal job had been in the Navy Department. He had always believed in the importance of a powerful Navy and had done everything in his power to improve and strengthen it. As a result of his efforts, 16 new battleships were built following the Spanish-American War of 1898, at a rate of almost two a year. Finally, in 1907, Roosevelt felt that the U.S. Navy had reached a peak of size and strength. He wanted to test its efficiency—and also to show it off to the rest of the world.

The Navy of 1907 was sometimes called the Great White

Fleet, because the ships had been painted white. In December of that year, a fleet of naval ships gathered at a port called Capes of the Chesapeake, in Virginia, under Admiral Robley D. Evans. On his own initiative, without asking Congress, Roosevelt ordered the fleet on a round-the-world cruise. The ships steamed first around the tip of South America and north through the Pacific to Japan. Then they continued westward through the China Sea, the Indian Ocean, the Suez Canal, the Mediterranean Sea, and the Atlantic Ocean.

The trip was a practical and popular success. Not only did the fleet keep to schedule and demonstrate the effectiveness of naval power for long-range operations around the world, but it was greeted with enthusiasm and respect everywhere it went. Americans were proud to read in the newspapers of their Great White Fleet's splendid showing in the ports of the world. In February of 1909, after 14 months and 45,000 miles at sea, the fleet returned to Virginia. It had established the United States as second only to England as a naval power. It was a proud moment for Roosevelt, the champion of naval strength.

The Gift of Inspiration

One of Roosevelt's greatest services to his country was the way he drew many capable and brilliant people into public service. He had the ability to recognize talent and to see where and how it could best be used. He also possessed the gift of inspiring in other people, through his vigorous speeches and conversations and through his writings, the desire to serve their country.

Among the many people Roosevelt appointed to public office were three Supreme Court justices: William R. Day, William H. Moody, and Oliver Wendell Holmes. Holmes was especially important in the history of the Supreme Court. After his appointment to the Court in 1902, he served for 30 years. Holmes is generally regarded as one of the most thoughtful, literate, and high-principled justices ever to serve on the Supreme Court. Many of the decisions he wrote are considered landmarks of American law.

Roosevelt's gift for inspiring and attracting earnest and capable public servants was widely recognized in his own time. James Bryce, the British ambassador to Washington, said that he had "never in any country seen a more eager, high-minded, and efficient set of public servants, men more useful and creditable to their country, than the men doing the work of the American Government."

Chapter 7

Later Years

As Roosevelt's second term drew to a close, he began to regret his promise not to run again for the presidency. He was popular with the majority of Americans, who believed that he had boosted the prestige of the United States among the nations of the world and had fought for the rights of ordinary people at home.

The newspapers devoted much space to Roosevelt's proclamations and actions; "Teddy," or "TR," was a familiar figure in the headlines and cartoons of the time. He was so well known and well liked that after a hunting trip on which he spared the life of a young bear cub, a cartoonist portrayed the incident in a drawing that was reproduced many times. Toymakers then began producing stuffed baby bears that became known as Teddy bears.

In short, although many congressmen were less than happy with his overbearing and forceful ways, Roosevelt knew that he could probably win the Republican nomination and the election. But he kept his promise and did not run. Instead, he lent his support to the campaign of William Howard Taft, who was his secretary of war. Taft was elected in 1908, and Roosevelt left the White House in early 1909. He was 50 years old at the time.

During a hunting trip to Mississippi in 1902, Roosevelt spared the life of a bear cub. The incident was widely portrayed in cartoons and pictures, and toymakers cashed in on Roosevelt's popularity to market "Teddy bears"—toys that still bear the President's name. (Library of Congress.)

FIRST RETIREMENT FROM POLITICS

After leaving Washington, Roosevelt spent some time at Sagamore Hill with his wife and family. But he was too energetic a man to settle into a quiet retirement at an early age. He decided to put his lifelong love of natural history and hunting to use in a new place: Africa. In mid-1909, he and his son Kermit, along with scientists and taxidermists from the Smithsonian Institution in Washington, set off on safari.

Roosevelt (standing) and his son Kermit (in the light helmet on the left) explored East Africa on a 10-month safari. They shot and preserved hundreds of animals and birds for Washington's Smithsonian Institution. (Library of Congress.)

They started in Mombasa, a port city on the Indian Ocean, and spent the next 10 months moving northward. As they went, they shot and prepared specimens of nearly 300 animals. About 260 porters were needed to carry the expedition's provisions, scientific equipment, and stuffed carcasses. The careful and intelligent notes Roosevelt made during the safari added considerably to the world's knowledge of African wildlife and geography. Even professional scientists agreed that he was a good naturalist.

The safari took Roosevelt to some of the wildest and most beautiful parts of East Africa: Mount Kenya, Lake Victoria, and the eastern corner of the Belgian Congo. In February of 1910, he arrived in The Sudan, a country sandwiched between Egypt and Ethiopia. There Edith Roosevelt joined her husband and son, and the three of them made a long, leisurely trip home together.

Along the way, Roosevelt made speeches at embassies and universities in The Sudan and in Cairo, Egypt, and then went on to Europe. He visited Rome and Paris, and he called on the rulers of Germany, Holland, Belgium, and Italy. King Edward VII of England died at this time, and at the request of President Taft, Roosevelt served as the official United States representative to the royal funeral. He also picked up his Nobel Peace Prize in Scandinavia and then lectured at England's Oxford and Cambridge universities.

One event of Roosevelt's stay in England was long remembered with amazement and admiration by the British. The former President passed the time one day by taking a stroll through New Forest, which is outside London, with Sir Edward Grey. Roosevelt the naturalist demonstrated that although he had spent only a few weeks in England since his boyhood, he could unfailingly identify every English bird and birdcall in the forest.

Roosevelt wanted to run for re-election in 1912, but despite support from many parts of the country, he did not receive the Republican Party's nomination. Never easily discouraged, he promptly formed his own party, the Progressive or Bull Moose Party. He lost the election to Woodrow Wilson and the Demo-crats. (Library of Congress.)

RETURN TO POLITICS

Upon his return to the United States, Roosevelt received a tumultuous welcome that reminded him of his personal popularity. He was aware once again that he might have had a third term in the White House. At the same time, he was disappointed in Taft's administration.

Taft had become very cautious and conservative. He discouraged rapid growth and counteracted some of Roosevelt's favorite conservation policies. Even Roosevelt's chief forester, Gifford Pinchot, had been forced to resign from the National Conservation Commission because of his repeated disagreements with Taft's administration. Some less conservative members of the Republican Party—those who favored Roosevelt's policies of vigorous growth and reform—asked the former President if he would consider running in the 1912 campaign.

Roosevelt agreed to think it over. For the next several years, in speeches and articles, he promoted what he called "the new nationalism." Its principles were social justice and control of government institutions by the people. It became clear that Roosevelt was using the new nationalism to pave the way for a presidential platform. Finally, Republicans who were at odds with Taft persuaded Roosevelt to declare his candidacy in February of 1912.

But Roosevelt did not triumph at the Republican National Convention. Taft was renominated, in spite of widespread support for Roosevelt among the American people. However, Roosevelt had worked too hard and gone too far to back down now. He and his backers promptly formed a new political party, the Progressive Party. At its convention in Chicago in August of 1912, the Progressive Party nominated Roosevelt as its presidential candidate. When a reporter asked him how he felt about the coming fight at the polls, Roosevelt answered bluffly, "I am as fit as a bull moose." The Progressive Party was quickly nicknamed the Bull Moose Party.

Assassination Attempt

That fitness was gravely challenged a few months later, in October. As Roosevelt prepared to make a speech in Milwaukee, he was shot once in the chest. The bullet was slowed when it passed through the thick speech he carried in his breast pocket and struck his metal spectacle case. Roosevelt was not killed, only injured. Despite his injury, he dramatically insisted on delivering his speech as planned. Only after he had addressed the crowd for more than an hour would he agree to go to the hospital.

Roosevelt recovered thoroughly and rapidly. His would-be assassin, a German immigrant house painter named Richard Schrank, explained to the authorities that he had seen the ghost of William McKinley in a dream, and that the ghost had told Schrank to kill Roosevelt in revenge for McKinley's own assassination. Schrank was declared insane; he died in a mental home in 1943.

When election time came in November, both Roosevelt and Taft were bitterly disappointed. The existence of two rival candidates split the Republican Party and the Republican vote, giving neither candidate a majority. Woodrow Wilson, the Democratic candidate, was elected. Many Republicans felt that Roosevelt's insistence on running as a third-party candidate had killed the party's chances. Warren G. Harding remarked in disgust, "Well, the mad Roosevelt has a new achievement to his credit. He succeeded in defeating the party that furnished him a job for nearly all of his manhood days after leaving the ranch."

SECOND RETIREMENT

Roosevelt's defeat as the Bull Moose candidate in 1912 marked the real end of his political career. He was asked by the Progressive Party to run again in 1916, but he refused. By this time, he had decided that unity among the Republicans was better than splitting the vote between Republicans and Progressives. So he supported the 1916 Republican candidate, Charles Evans Hughes, who lost to Wilson.

Before 1916, however, Roosevelt had turned his attention to other activities. He wrote many newspaper and magazine articles and several books, including his autobiography, which was published in 1913. He lived the life of a country gentleman at Sagamore Hill, enjoying the company of his growing children. One incident of 1913 gave him great amusement: he sued a magazine editor who had written that Roosevelt was often drunk. Roosevelt mustered dozens of character witnesses and descended with them upon the small Michigan town where the trial was held. The witnesses attested to Roosevelt's sobriety, and the sheepish editor was forced to admit that he did not have a drop of evidence to support his statement. After Roosevelt won the case, he good-naturedly asked for only six cents in damages.

The River of Doubt

Later that year, Roosevelt embarked on another epic journey of exploration and discovery. In October, he and Kermit went to Brazil to collect birds and animals for the American Museum of Natural History, which Roosevelt's father had helped start. A Brazilian explorer, Colonel Candido Rondon, suggested to Roosevelt that they should chart the course of an unexplored river in the Brazilian jungles that was known only as the River of Doubt.

The expedition turned out to be a grueling test of stamina and determination. The party made a journey of more than 1,000 miles through unmapped wilderness, in constant danger of starvation or attack by hostile Indians. The river was a mass of rapids and whirlpools, and Roosevelt's leg was injured when he tried to save a boat that had capsized. The injury became infected, fever set in, and then Roosevelt was stricken with malaria.

The rest of the party gallantly struggled onward with the sick and injured Roosevelt. They were at the end of their strength and their supplies when, at last, they emerged into civilization. The river they had been following flowed into the Madeira River, along which there were towns. The Madeira, in turn, flowed into the mighty Amazon River. The party obtained vital supplies and traveled downriver by boat to safety. The world applauded Roosevelt's courage, and Brazil showed its admiration for his achievement by renaming the River of Doubt. It became the Rio Roosevelt.

War and Tragedy

Roosevelt returned to Sagamore Hill in May of 1914. Later that year, in August, World War I broke out in Europe. At first, Roosevelt tried to maintain a neutral position. Within a few weeks, however, he was urging the United States to join the war on the side of England and France. He did not want Germany to win because victory would give that country control of British possessions in Canada and the Caribbean, and he felt that Germany's warlike tendencies would eventually draw it into war with the United States in the New World.

Roosevelt also felt that German methods of warfare — such as its attack on a civilian ship, the *Lusitania* — were barbaric. In speeches and articles, he condemned the cautious policies of the Wilson administration and tried to rouse his countrymen to fight an honorable war: "Let us pay with our bodies for our souls' desire!" he cried.

Roosevelt was glad that the United States finally entered the war in 1917. He asked Wilson for permission to form a volunteer force to be called the Roosevelt Division—a sort of enlarged version of the old Rough Riders—but the President refused, preferring to leave the fighting to the regular armed forces. "This is a very exclusive war," Roosevelt said wryly after his offer was turned down, "and I have been black-balled by the committee on admissions."

All four of Roosevelt's sons served in battle. Theodore, Jr., an exact image of his father in appearance and habits, commanded an infantry regiment at the Argonne, in France, and won a Purple Heart, a Distinguished Service Medal, and a Distinguished Service Cross. Kermit was a major in the artillery (cannon and guns). Archibald, an Army captain, was discharged after being severely wounded in France; he received the French *Croix de Guerre* (Cross of Battle). But the tragedy of the war for the Roosevelt family concerned the youngest child, Quentin, who was a pilot in the Army Air Corps. He was shot down and killed over France in 1918.

Quentin's death was a source of great sorrow to Roosevelt, yet the former President remained proud of his sons' response to their country's call to arms. "It is very dreadful that he should have been killed," Roosevelt said. "It would have been worse if he had not gone."

The former President did what he could to help the war effort at home, despite periods of illness from his Brazilian leg injury and fevers, and also from an ear infection that left him partly deaf. He toured the country making speeches on behalf of the Red Cross and the sale of war bonds.

His injuries and illnesses were wearing out even Roosevelt's legendary vitality. In 1918, he began to suffer from a painful form of rheumatism that caused his joints to become inflamed. He grew weak. But the end was nearer than he or his family suspected.

On January 5, 1919, Roosevelt worked at home on an editorial for the *Kansas City Star*, then went to bed. His last words, addressed to a servant, were, "Please put out the light." He died in his sleep that night of a blood clot in his heart; he was 60 years old.

Roosevelt's funeral service, held in Oyster Bay, was simple and quiet, as he had requested. He was buried there, near Sagamore Hill. After his death, Edith Roosevelt traveled around the world and spent much time with her children and, eventually, her grandchildren. She died at Sagamore Hill at the age of 87, and was buried next to her husband.

MEMORIALS TO ROOSEVELT

Theodore Roosevelt's memory has been kept alive in many forms. Thousands of people have read his books about history, politics, and adventure. His sister Corinne wrote a popular book called *My Brother, Theodore Roosevelt* in 1921, and scores of other books have been written about him. A river in South America and a dam in Arizona bear his name, as do many sites and features in the United States national park system, which he helped to create. One special part of that system is the Theodore Roosevelt National Park, established in North Dakota in 1947. It contains the Elkhorn Ranch, where Roosevelt learned to be a cowboy.

In Washington, D.C., the Potomac River—in which Roosevelt used to swim summer and winter—flows around a speck of land called Theodore Roosevelt Island. A large statue on the island commemorates the former President. But a much grander memorial is located in South Dakota, in the wild country that Roosevelt loved. It is Mount Rushmore National Memorial.

Roosevelt is one of four Presidents whose 60-foot-high faces were carved into the granite mountain by Danish-born sculptor Gutzon Borglum between 1927 and 1941. The other Presidents memorialized on Mount Rushmore are George Washington (the nation's founder), Thomas Jefferson (the nation's philosopher), and Abraham Lincoln (who restored the nation's unity).

Roosevelt had been dead for less than a decade when the work at Mount Rushmore was begun, and some people complained that he did not deserve to be included among the four greatest Presidents the country had known. But he was included—a decision that most Americans supported—because he had given the nation its proud place among the countries of the world. And he was, as President Calvin Coolidge reminded America, "the first President who had actively worked to protect the rights of the working man."

Theodore Roosevelt has passed into history as one of the most strong-willed, energetic, and optimistic Presidents the United States has known. His life and his presidency were guided by values that appealed to the majority of Americans of his time: honesty, pride, belief in the responsibility of government to protect the weak, and great admiration for courage and strength—when that strength was used for good. More than any other President, he made the United States into a world power, but he strove always to use that power honorably.

Bibliography

Beach, James Caleb. *Theodore Roosevelt, Man of Action.* Champaign, Illinois: Garrard Press, 1960. This very short and simple book for younger readers focuses on the active side of Roosevelt's career, especially the charge up San Juan Hill.

Beale, Howard Kennedy. *Theodore Roosevelt and the Rise of America to World Power.* Baltimore: Johns Hopkins Press, 1956. At 600 pages, this may be more detailed than some readers want, but it is a thorough account of how Roosevelt affected the United States' position in the world during his lifetime and ever since.

Blum, John Morton. *The Republican Roosevelt.* New York: Atheneum, 1962. This short, readable volume concentrates on Roosevelt's relationship with the Republican Party—his squabbles with party bosses, his triumphs, and his failure to secure the 1912 presidential nomination.

Chessman, G. Wallace. *Theodore Roosevelt and the Politics of Power.* Boston: Little, Brown, 1969. This book is about Roosevelt's "Big Stick" theory and the ways he put it into practice. Chessman is fair in pointing out both the positive and negative aspects of Big Stick diplomacy.

Emerson, Edwin. *Adventures of Theodore Roosevelt.* New York: Dutton, 1928. Written not long after Roosevelt's death, this biography has a hero-worshipping tone but is entertaining for its accounts of Roosevelt on the ranch, on safari, and in the jungle.

Hagedorn, Hermann. *The Roosevelt Family of Sagamore Hill.* New York: Macmillan, 1954. Hagedorn discusses Theodore Roosevelt's ancestors, parents, wives, children, and descendants, while painting a colorful picture of life at the Roosevelt estate on Long Island.

Harbaugh, William H. *Power and Responsibility: The Life and Times of Theodore Roosevelt.* New York: Oxford University Press, 1961; revised edition, 1975. This book is another look at the Big Stick method of international politics. It also examines Roosevelt's life and his belief that powerful nations like the United States had a responsibility to use their power fairly and helpfully.

McCullough, David G. *Mornings on Horseback.* New York: Simon and Schuster, 1981. This 445-page account of Roosevelt's family, childhood, youth, and early life was a best-seller when it appeared. It is lively and entertaining, and it draws on many letters and memoirs of the Roosevelt clan.

Morris, Edmund. *The Rise of Theodore Roosevelt.* New York: Coward, McCann, and Geoghegan, 1979. This lengthy (886 pages) account of Roosevelt's rise to national importance covers his early political career, his involvement in New York State politics, and his work in New York City and the Navy Department.

Pringle, Henry F. *Theodore Roosevelt: A Biography.* New York: Harcourt, Brace, Jovanovich, 1956. This is a good, basic, general-purpose biography.

Robinson, Corinne Roosevelt. *My Brother, Theodore Roosevelt.* New York: Scribner's, 1921. Two years after her brother's death, Roosevelt's sister published this account of his life and personality. Although it is neither complete nor objective, it is worth reading for the picture it paints of the brilliant Roosevelt clan and their interesting, important lives.

Roosevelt, Theodore. *An Autobiography.* New York: Macmillan, 1914. It is probably true that we should never base our final judgment of a statesman on what he says about himself. Roosevelt's autobiography, like all such books, is biased by lack of perspective and the desire to justify the author's own opinions and actions. Nevertheless, it is fascinating reading and shows Roosevelt's power to captivate and charm an audience. It is also a valuable source of inside information.

Roosevelt, Theodore. *Hunting Trips of a Ranchman and Hunting Trips on the Prairies and in the Mountains.* New York: Review of Reviews, 1904. No one could tell Teddy Roosevelt's stories better than Teddy himself. This volume contains reprints of two of his books about hunting adventures in the West. They show his love of both strenuous physical activity and the great outdoors.

Index

PRESIDENTS OF THE UNITED STATES

GEORGE WASHINGTON	L. Falkof	0-944483-19-4
JOHN ADAMS	R. Stefoff	0-944483-10-0
THOMAS JEFFERSON	R. Stefoff	0-944483-07-0
JAMES MADISON	B. Polikoff	0-944483-22-4
JAMES MONROE	R. Stefoff	0-944483-11-9
JOHN QUINCY ADAMS	M. Greenblatt	0-944483-21-6
ANDREW JACKSON	R. Stefoff	0-944483-08-9
MARTIN VAN BUREN	R. Ellis	0-944483-12-7
WILLIAM HENRY HARRISON	R. Stefoff	0-944483-54-2
JOHN TYLER	L. Falkof	0-944483-60-7
JAMES K. POLK	M. Greenblatt	0-944483-04-6
ZACHARY TAYLOR	D. Collins	0-944483-17-8
MILLARD FILLMORE	K. Law	0-944483-61-5
FRANKLIN PIERCE	F. Brown	0-944483-25-9
JAMES BUCHANAN	D. Collins	0-944483-62-3
ABRAHAM LINCOLN	R. Stefoff	0-944483-14-3
ANDREW JOHNSON	R. Stevens	0-944483-16-X
ULYSSES S. GRANT	L. Falkof	0-944483-02-X
RUTHERFORD B. HAYES	N. Robbins	0-944483-23-2
JAMES A. GARFIELD	F. Brown	0-944483-63-1
CHESTER A. ARTHUR	R. Stevens	0-944483-05-4
GROVER CLEVELAND	D. Collins	0-944483-01-1
BENJAMIN HARRISON	R. Stevens	0-944483-15-1
WILLIAM McKINLEY	D. Collins	0-944483-55-0
THEODORE ROOSEVELT	R. Stefoff	0-944483-09-7
WILLIAM H. TAFT	L. Falkof	0-944483-56-9
WOODROW WILSON	D. Collins	0-944483-18-6
WARREN G. HARDING	A. Canadeo	0-944483-64-X
CALVIN COOLIDGE	R. Stevens	0-944483-57-7

HERBERT C. HOOVER	B. Polikoff	0-944483-58-5
FRANKLIN D. ROOSEVELT	M. Greenblatt	0-944483-06-2
HARRY S. TRUMAN	D. Collins	0-944483-00-3
DWIGHT D. EISENHOWER	R. Ellis	0-944483-13-5
JOHN F. KENNEDY	L. Falkof	0-944483-03-8
LYNDON B. JOHNSON	L. Falkof	0-944483-20-8
RICHARD M. NIXON	R. Stefoff	0-944483-59-3
GERALD R. FORD	D. Collins	0-944483-65-8
JAMES E. CARTER	D. Richman	0-944483-24-0
RONALD W. REAGAN	N. Robbins	0-944483-66-6
GEORGE H.W. BUSH	R. Stefoff	1-56074-033-7
WILLIAM J. CLINTON	D. Collins	1-56074-056-6

GARRETT EDUCATIONAL CORPORATION
130 EAST 13TH STREET
ADA, OK 74820